T0297395

Building a Practical Information Security Program

Building a Practical Information Security Program

Jason Andress, CISSP, ISSAP, CISM, GPEN

Mark Leary, CISSP, CISM, CGIET, PMP

AMSTERDAM • BOSTON • CAMBRIDGE • HEIDELBERG • LONDON
NEW YORK • OXFORD • PARIS • SAN DIEGO
SAN FRANCISCO • SINGAPORE • SYDNEY • TOKYO

Syngress is an imprint of Elsevier

SYNGRESS.

Syngress is an imprint of Elsevier
50 Hampshire Street, 5th Floor, Cambridge, MA 02139, United States

Notices
Knowledge and best practice in this field are constantly changing. As new research and experience broaden our understanding, changes in research methods, professional practices, or medical treatment may become necessary.

Practitioners and researchers must always rely on their own experience and knowledge in evaluating and using any information, methods, compounds, or experiments described herein. In using such information or methods they should be mindful of their own safety and the safety of others, including parties for whom they have a professional responsibility.

To the fullest extent of the law, neither the Publisher nor the authors, contributors, or editors, assume any liability for any injury and/or damage to persons or property as a matter of products liability, negligence or otherwise, or from any use or operation of any methods, products, instructions, or ideas contained in the material herein.

Library of Congress Cataloging-in-Publication Data
A catalog record for this book is available from the Library of Congress

British Library Cataloguing-in-Publication Data
A catalogue record for this book is available from the British Library

ISBN: 978-0-12-802042-5

For information on all Syngress publications
visit our website at https://www.elsevier.com/

Working together
to grow libraries in
developing countries

www.elsevier.com • www.bookaid.org

Publisher: Todd Green
Acquisition Editor: Chris Katsaropoulos
Editorial Project Manager: Anna Valutkevich
Production Project Manager: Priya Kumaraguruparan
Cover Designer: Matthew Limbert

Typeset by TNQ Books and Journals

Contents

About the Authors

JASON ANDRESS

Jason Andress (ISSAP, CISSP, GPEN, CEH) is a seasoned security professional with a depth of experience in both the academic and business worlds. Presently he carries out information security oversight duties, performing penetration testing, risk assessment, and compliance functions to ensure that critical assets are protected. Jason has taught undergraduate and graduate security courses since 2005 and holds a doctorate in computer science, researching in the area of data protection. He has authored several publications and books, writing on topics including data security, network security, penetration testing, and digital forensics.

MARK LEARY

Mark Leary possesses over 30 years of experience in security management and technical intelligence holding several positions of responsibility in IT security management for government agencies and commercial firms. Mark currently performs as Vice President and Chief Information Security Officer for Xerox Corporation, the world's leading global enterprise for business process and document management with sales approaching $23 billion. Marks holds a Doctorate in Management, MBA with a concentration in Project Management, Dual Masters in Security and IT Management, and several professional certifications (CISSP, CISM, CGIET, and PMP). He also serves as an Adjunct Professor for the University of Maryland and Industry Advisor to the Rochester Institute of Technology.

Why We Need Security Programs

INFORMATION IN THIS CHAPTER:

- What do we mean when we say Information Security?
- Security focus areas
- Understanding the threats we face
- Benefits of a Formal Security Program
- Actions

As, a concept, information security becomes ever more a part of our societies. This is, in a large part, a result of our nearly ubiquitous adoption of computing technology. Many of us depend on computers in our everyday lives. We sit in front of computers for our employers, we play on them at home, we go to school online, and we buy goods from merchants on the Internet. Our laptops go with us to the coffee shop so we can check our e-mail and do homework. We carry our smartphones at all times so we can check our bank balances on the go. We read and watch movies on our iPads. The sensors on our wrists track the calories we burn and hours we sleep.

These technologies enable us to be more productive and access a host of information with only a click of the mouse, but they also bring with them a large set of security issues. If the information on the systems used by our employers or our banks becomes exposed to an attacker, the consequences can be dire indeed. Our business may suddenly find itself bereft of funds, as the contents of its accounts are transferred to a bank in another country in the middle of the night. Our employer could lose millions of dollars, face legal prosecution, and suffer damage to its reputation because of a system configuration issue allowing an attacker to gain access to a database containing personally identifiable information or proprietary information. Such issues appear in the media with disturbing regularity.

If we look back 30 years, such issues related to computer systems were nearly nonexistent, largely due to the low level of technology and the few people

1

Building a Practical Information Security Program. http://dx.doi.org/10.1016/B978-0-12-802042-5.00001-9

who were using what was in place to run our business or finances. Although technology changes at an increasingly rapid rate, and specific implementations arise on a seemingly daily basis, much of the theory that discusses how we go about keeping ourselves secure changes at a much slower pace because it involves the underlying protocols and infrastructure and does not always keep up with the changes to our technology. If we can gain a good understanding of the basics of information security and how to apply them, we are on a strong footing to cope with changes as they come along.

WHAT DO WE MEAN WHEN WE SAY INFORMATION SECURITY?

Information security is defined as "protecting information and information systems from unauthorized access, use, disclosure, disruption, modification, or destruction," according to US law [1]. In essence, it means we want to protect our data and the systems that hold it from those who would seek to misuse it.

In a general sense, security means protecting our assets. This may mean protecting them from attackers invading our networks, natural disasters, adverse environmental conditions, power failures, theft or vandalism, or other undesirable states. Ultimately, we will attempt to secure ourselves against the most likely forms of attack, to the best extent we reasonably can, given our environment and tolerance for risk.

When we look at what exactly it is that we secure, we may have a broad range of potential assets. We can consider physical items that we might want to secure, such as those of inherent value (e.g., gold bullion) or those that have value to our business (e.g., computing hardware). We may also have items of a more ethereal nature, such as software, source code, or data. In today's computing environment, we are likely to find that our logical assets are at least as valuable as, if not more than, our physical assets. In addition, we must also protect the people who are involved in our operations. People are our single most valuable asset, as we cannot generally conduct business without them. We duplicate our physical and logical assets and keep backup copies of them elsewhere against catastrophe occurring, but without the skilled people to operate and maintain our environments, we will swiftly fail.

In our efforts to secure our assets, we must also consider the consequences of the security we choose to implement. Although we could certainly say that a system in such a state could be considered reasonably secure, it is surely not usable or productive. As we increase the level of security, we usually decrease the level of productivity. With the system mentioned in our quote, the level of security would be very high, but the level of productivity would be very near zero; it is key to find the right balance.

In addition, when securing an asset, system, or environment, we must also consider how the level of security relates to the value of the item being secured. We can, if we are willing to accommodate the decrease in performance, apply very high levels of security to every asset for which we are responsible. We can build a billion-dollar facility surrounded by razor wire fences and patrolled by armed guards and vicious attack dogs, and carefully place our asset in a hermetically sealed vault inside…so that mom's chocolate chip cookie recipe will never come to harm, but that would not make much sense. In some environments, however, such security measures might not be enough. In any environment where we plan to put heightened levels of security in place, we also need to take into account the cost of replacing our assets if we do happen to lose them, and make sure we establish reasonable levels of protection for their value. The cost of the security we put in place should never outstrip the value of what it is protecting.

Confidentiality, Integrity, and Availability Triad

Three of the primary concepts in information security are confidentiality, integrity, and availability, commonly known as the confidentiality, integrity, and availability (CIA) triad, as shown in Fig. 0.1. The CIA triad gives us a model by which we can think about and discuss security concepts, and tends to be very focused on security, as it pertains to data.

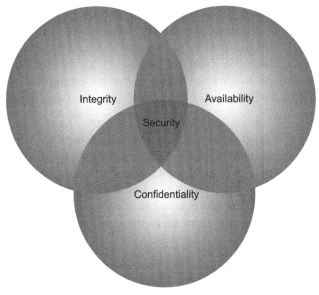

FIGURE 0.1
CIA triad.

Confidentiality

Confidentiality is a concept similar to, but not the same as, privacy. Confidentiality is a necessary component of privacy and refers to our ability to protect our data from those who are not authorized to view it. Confidentiality is a concept that may be implemented at many levels of a process.

As an example, if we consider the case of a person withdrawing money from an automated teller machine (ATM), the person in question will likely seek to maintain the confidentiality of the personal identification number (PIN) that allows him, in combination with his ATM card, to draw funds from the ATM. In addition, the owner of the ATM will hopefully maintain the confidentiality of the account number, balance, and any other information needed to communicate to the bank from which the funds are being drawn. The bank will maintain the confidentiality of the transaction with the ATM and the balance change in the account after the funds have been withdrawn. If at any point in the transaction confidentiality is compromised, the results could be bad for the individual, the owner of the ATM, and the bank, potentially resulting in what is known in the information security field as a breach.

Confidentiality can be compromised by the loss of a laptop containing data, a person looking over our shoulder while we type a password, an e-mail attachment being sent to the wrong person, an attacker penetrating our systems, or similar issues.

Integrity

Integrity refers to the ability to prevent our data from being changed in an unauthorized or undesirable manner. This could mean the unauthorized change or deletion of our data or portions of our data, or it could mean an authorized, but undesirable, change or deletion of our data. To maintain integrity, we not only need to have the means to prevent unauthorized changes to our data but also need the ability to reverse authorized changes that need to be undone.

We can see a good example of mechanisms that allow us to control integrity in the file systems of many modern operating systems such as Windows and Linux. For purposes of preventing unauthorized changes, such systems often implement permissions that restrict what actions an unauthorized user can perform on a given file. In addition, some such systems, and many applications, such as databases, can allow us to undo or roll back changes that are undesirable.

Integrity is particularly important when we are discussing the data that provide the foundation for other decisions. If an attacker were to alter the data that contained the results of medical tests, we might see the wrong treatment prescribed, potentially resulting in the death of the patient.

Integrity can be compromised on purpose or by accident by modifying the data on which our business depends. The data entry clerk who misplaces a decimal point when changing the price of a product can do just as much damage as an attacker that hacks in to modify the same data. Some may also argue that accidental modification of data extends into a question of validity.

Availability

The final leg of the CIA triad is availability. Availability refers to the ability to access our data when we need it. Loss of availability can refer to a wide variety of breaks anywhere in the chain that allows us access to our data. Such issues can result from power loss, operating system or application problems, network attacks, compromise of a system, denial of connectivity, or other problems. When such issues are caused by an outside party, such as an attacker, they are commonly referred to as a denial of service (DoS) attack and can be against end devices or the bandwidth to support them.

Relating the CIA Triad to Security

Given the elements of the CIA triad, we can begin to discuss security issues in a very specific fashion. As an example, we can look at a shipment of backup media on which we have the only existing, but unencrypted, copy of some of our sensitive data stored. If we were to lose the shipment in transit, we will have a security issue. From a confidentiality standpoint, we are likely to have a problem since our files were not encrypted. From an integrity standpoint, presuming that we were able to recover the tapes, we again have an issue due to the lack of encryption used on our files. If we recover the tapes and the unencrypted files were altered, this would not be immediately apparent to us. As for availability, we have an issue unless the tapes are recovered since we do not have a backup copy of the files.

Availability can be compromised by any event that prevents us from important resources. A good example of this is ransomware—malware that encrypts data with a key known only to the attacker, with the express purpose in mind of extorting funds from the victim in exchange for revealing the encryption key so that the victim can reclaim their files.

Compliance and Risk

Another important concept to address is that of compliance versus risk. With the natural difficulty of determining what an appropriate level of security investment is some security programs are developed with the idea in mind of "checking the box" to satisfy the auditors that are assessing the organization's degree of compliance with the various regulations and requirements under which they operate. Although this level of security may scrape through an audit and satisfy the paper requirement for security, it by no means constitutes an actual security program. In the case where a company that has been determined to be compliant with whatever standard(s) they are being held to is breached, the situation may descend into a maelstrom of accusals, counter accusals, and lawsuits, as each party attempts to be the one that is not to blame. Clearly, this is an undesirable situation.

As discussed later, two general approaches to building security programs are the above-mentioned compliance-based program and a risk-based approach. The risk-based approach, although almost definitely resulting in a stronger program (which as compliance as a subset), is also more resource intensive and may not apply well to all organizations, particularly those that are very small in size, or on very tight resource constraints.

Compliance Based

In recent years various compliance requirements have greatly changed the way that the information security industry, and the businesses and organizations which it supports, has begun to operate. If we look back a decade, the majority of information security efforts were centered on a few policies and a general mandate to keep attackers out. Yes, regulations did exist at that time to help protect data and consumers, but such efforts were considerably less defined than they are now and not as strictly enforced.

In the present state of the security industry, we have a number of issues that force us more in the direction of compliance. There are a seemingly ever increasing number of large breaches, the Target breach in December of 2013 https://paperpile.com/c/cTAM8E/0PJ9 [1] being a very public example of such, which draw additional scrutiny to compliance issues (PCI in this case). There are also regular updates to the regulations with which we must comply and new regulations being enacted. This creates a moving target for companies that need to be concerned with compliance.

Given the set of regulations and industry requirements that we might be required to comply with while operating in any given industry, it can be easy for an organization to become trapped by these requirements when developing a program. If we allow our program to organically develop, tacking things on in a reactionary way as we encounter compliance requirements, specific issues, audit findings, and other such drivers, we will likely end up with a very unbalanced program.

Compliance requirements are not meant to take the place of intentionally developing a sound foundation for information security. They exist to set minimum standards for, in most cases, protecting the customers that we serve.

Risk Based

Risk-based security programs represent the more planned and intentional methodology for constructing a security program. At a high level, a risk-based program is developed by identifying our important assets, identifying the

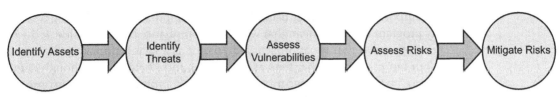

FIGURE 0.2
Risk mitigation process.

potential threats against them, assessing the vulnerabilities that we have present, and then taking steps to mitigate these risks, as shown in Fig. 0.2.

In building a security program based on actual risks that pertain to our environment, we build not just a generic security program, but a program that is suited to our particular needs.

First and foremost, we need to conduct a security assessment for our organization. The rest of the program flows from this assessment. Using the National Institute of Standards and Technology (NIST) SP800-30 https://paperpile.com/c/cTAM8E/QWeV [2] as a basis, the assessment should include the following items:

- System characterization
- Threat identification
- Vulnerability identification
- Control analysis
- Likelihood determination
- Impact analysis
- Risk determination
- Control recommendations
- Results documentation

TIP

The NIST produces a number of Special Publications that provide government agencies with guidance on a variety of technical topics, including information security. NIST SP800-30 is the Guide for Conduct Risk Assessments. The list of Special Publications can be found at http://csrc.nist.gov/publications/PubsSPs.html and is a very useful source of guidance when developing the various parts of a security program.

With the risk assessment in hand, we can begin to lay out a roadmap that addresses the operational, tactical, and strategic goals of our organization. Given these goals, we can then forecast the required resources to accomplish these goals and use this as the basis for management discussions around the controls that we need to put in place, a security budget, and a number of other such details.

It is important to note that using a risk-based approach to developing a security program does not mean that we throw compliance by the wayside. It does, however, mean that we approach compliance as a factor in making decisions about our program, rather than as the driving force behind it. Although compliance may not equal security, security done properly should encompass compliance.

SECURITY FOCUS AREAS

When we look at the security program, there are a number of levels at which we can focus, moving from the lowest and most in the weeds technical details at the tactical level, to very-high-level national security issues at the most strategic level. Each of these focus areas is necessary to getting the work of the security program done, and to ensuring that the work being done at that particular level is appropriate and effective. We have all experienced or heard of the manager at high or middle levels who is unable to leave the technical work efforts to those who are specifically employed to do said work, and insists on jogging the elbows of these poor souls. Likewise, asking our technical staff to make high-level strategic decisions can have equally disastrous results.

Looking at the focus areas in question, from tactical to strategic, we have: technical, management, board level, industry, and national, as shown in Fig. 0.3.

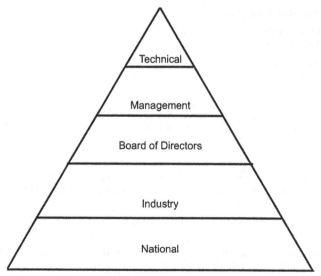

FIGURE 0.3
Security focus areas.

Technical

The technical level is at the most tactical end of the spectrum. The work that goes on here is where the rubber meets the security road. Here we have the architects, engineers, and analysts who are working to keep attackers out of our systems and are directly tuning the systems that keep our security infrastructure humming along properly. We may see the organization split into several teams at the technical level, to allow focus on specific efforts. We might commonly see divisions along the lines of engineering, operations, consulting, architecture, and penetration testing efforts. We may also see additional divisions along geographical boundaries. This will vary highly from one organization to another, depending on the specific needs and the size of the organization, and indeed the composition of such teams is very likely to change over time, even in a single organization.

They are architecting, implementing, and maintaining our critical security infrastructure like firewalls, Intrusion Detection Systems, Data Loss Prevention tools, and the many other capabilities that need to take place to keep our security infrastructure working. They are combatting malware that has infected our systems, responding to security incidents and investigating employee misconduct involving our computer systems, conducting forensic collections from systems and performing analysis on them, and a myriad of other such efforts on a daily basis.

Some portion of the personnel at this level may also be shift based, in the case of Incident Response or Security Operations Center personnel, who we might require to respond around the clock as issues arise. Others can be on call or respond as required.

We would typically not expect our people with a technical focus to be setting the overall direction for the program or working at a higher level of strategic concern, although this may be a portion of the duties asked of the architecture role in some organizations.

Management

At a management level of focus, at a high level, we should see the direction set for the overall security program. The particular duties carried out at the management level of focus will vary considerably from one organization to the next and will also depend to a certain extent on the management structure. We might typically see management reporting to middle management reporting to a chief information security officer (CISO) or, lacking a CISO, a chief information officer, who may then report to a chief executive/financial/operations officer, who will likely report to the board, as shown in Fig. 0.4.

FIGURE 0.4

Typical organization of security management. *CEO*, chief executive officer; *CFO*, chief financial officer; *CIO*, chief information officer; *CISO*, chief information security officer; *COO*, chief operations officer.

We would typically expect the CISO, or whoever is filling this role under a different title, to set the direction for the organization's overall security program. The CISO also has the ultimate responsibility for the success or failure of the program, and should set the vision and drive the culture of the organization. The CISO will also more than likely set the overall budget for the security organization and will sign off on very impactful security decisions. Because they are responsible they may find themselves in a precarious career position, should the program fail dramatically and publicly, in the case of a large breach that reaches the national news media.

Middle management in an information security is typically put in place to facilitate the smooth functioning of such organizations as they grow and mature. Past a certain point, it is not feasible for everyone in security to report directly to the CISO, and for this person to have a hand in every daily security decision.

Direct management of the technical teams, usually the first level or two of the structure, has a much more direct hand in how security functions for the organization. These managers are often setting specific budgets for purchases of security devices, making decisions for purchases directly, or requesting higher levels of management approval.

Board Level

At the level of the board of directors for the organization, information security concerns become largely indistinguishable from other business risks. If the business is not successful, then the security of the company and its information assets becomes somewhat of a moot point. For the business to succeed, we need to see to the overall security of the organization, protect customer data that are entrusted to us, and take care to safeguard our reputation. The CISO must present the information risks in a way the board can compare and evaluate what level of risk is appropriate to accept and where they should invest.

At a board level, the security of the organization revolves around the high-level successful completion of audits and similar external assessments, ensuring that we do not make the front page of the morning news by having a large or very public breach or security incident, and providing direction to the layers of management below to ensure that these things happen. In the last several years, cases where the board of directors was held responsible for security lapses in the security for the company that it oversees have become more common. Thus, ensuring that its members are not unwillingly fitted for orange jumpsuits is also a priority for the board. In addition, statements about cyber risk are becoming common in stockholder materials.

Protection of customer data is also an item of focus at the board level, as this refers directly to the above-mentioned breach issue. In a very large number of cases involving a breach of security or focused attack against a company, the target of the attack is customer information, often specifically stored customer payment card information. Even where this information is not directly present, customer personal information may still be the target, as this can be used to open fraudulent credit accounts in the name of the victim.

In addition, the board is focused on safeguarding the reputation of the company. All of the above-mentioned issues, when exposed to the public, represent damage to the reputation of the organization's brand. Although the public appears to have somewhat of a short-term memory as relates to the missteps of companies that have experienced such issues, repeated problems in this area will eventually begin to stick in the minds of the public.

Industry

At an industry level, the focus on security shifts to a much more broad focus than any one organization. An excellent example of this is that of the Payment Card Industry (PCI) Security Standards Council, developers of the PCI Data Security Standard (PCI DSS), Payment Application Data Security Standard, and PIN Transaction Security requirements. These standards are often collectively referred to as simply PCI.

This council was founded by the five major payment card brands: American Express, Discover Financial Services, JCB International, MasterCard, and Visa Inc. and exists to help ensure a consistent level of security among the customers who use the collective groups products, namely, anyone who takes a payment card as payment for good or services. For businesses to accept payment card transactions, they have to agree to abide by the PCI DSS and, with varying levels of scrutiny based on number of transactions, submit to yearly audits of their security programs.

WARNING

As discussed elsewhere in this chapter, meeting the bare minimum to ensure compliance with any of a number of standards, such as PCI DSS or HIPAA, does not equate to having a solid information security program. Although security can be seen as a superset of compliance, the reverse is not often true.

Via this mechanism, the PCI Security Standards Council influences industry level security for virtually anyone who uses payment cards as a portion of their business model. Similar comparisons can be made for other industry-focused security efforts, such as the Health Insurance Portability and Accountability Act (HIPAA), the North American Electric Reliability Corporation (NERC), and a host of others. We will discuss efforts such as these at a greater length in Chapter 2. We may also categorize HIPPA and NERC as being at a national level of focus as they really fit into both groups.

National

We might think that a national security level of focus would be strictly related to cyberwarfare and firmly in the realm of the various governmental agencies that concern themselves with such efforts, but this is not entirely the case.

NOTE

For an extensive overview of cybersecurity, cyberwarfare, and associate issues, see *Cyber Warfare: Techniques, Tactics and Tools for Security Practitioners* by Jason Andress and Steve Winterfeld, available from Syngress.

Although many of these matters are indeed above the level that an average organization would need to concern itself with, some are definitely still on our radar as security professionals. A large portion of the efforts of the Federal Bureau of Investigation (FBI) at this point are focused on cybercrime. Cybercriminals regularly attack businesses through theft of customer data and intellectual property, DoS attacks, fraud, malware, and any of a number of similar efforts.

The FBI, Federal Trade Commission, and US Secret Service are regularly involved in protecting US interests, including those of organizations that have attracted the attention of organized crime, black hat hackers, political activists, and other such parties.

Within our security organization, it often pays dividends to foster and develop relationships with the local representation of the agencies that are a part of combatting cybercrime on a national level. In several recent breach cases, the intrusions went undetected until they were reported by law enforcement agencies that were monitoring fraudulent and criminal activities on the part of the perpetrators.

UNDERSTANDING THE THREATS WE FACE

It is important when constructing a security program to understand the potential issues that we might face. Factors such as the motivations and intent of attackers, whether the threats are from external or internal attackers, or even risks brought about from the regulatory environments within which our particular industry operates may affect how we structure the security program for our organization.

Motivations and Intent

Understanding the motivations and intent of those who attack us can be of great assistance in planning how we will respond to them. How we handle these attacks can vary greatly from one situation to another.

For example, if we are operating in the financial industry, the financial assets that we are handling will likely present a very large target for attackers. If we are handling account numbers, customer information, and payment card numbers, these items are valuable to attackers from the standpoint of being saleable information. Likewise, websites and applications that allow customers to perform financial transactions such as moving money from one account or bank to another, sending wire transfers, or withdrawing money from retirement accounts present tempting targets to fraudsters and thieves. The motivations and intent here both sync up to being theft of inherently valuable information and our program and sets of controls will likely be very focused around keeping these particular assets safe.

In a different case, we might be developing a security program for a legal firm that handles civil rights cases for minorities and immigrants in troubled areas. Although we still have some similarities in that there is likely to be customer information present and, potentially, payment information, the same focus on protecting this is not present. In this case, we might need to worry about protecting customer information for matters of personal safety on the part of our clients, rather than financial issues. We could also potentially run up against attacks on our online presence, such as website defacement or DoS attacks on our email servers. Here the motivation and intent are both in the direction of preventing our services from be conducted and potentially harming us or our clients.

Two very different situations lead to different focus in our security program, different controls in place, and a generally different focus. Although the set of tools and resources needed to carry out both efforts would be largely the same, the application of it would be rather different.

External Threats

When we think of threats to organizations, many of us picture dimly lit and smoke-filled rooms populated by black hat hackers banging away at their keyboards as they chug highly caffeinated beverages, the stuff of cheesy hacker movies like Hackers and Swordfish.

> **NOTE**
>
> If you are unfamiliar with these movies, you are really missing out on a foundational bit of security knowledge. There are any number of lists https://paperpile.com/c/cTAM8E/aXE6 [3] of greatest hacker movies on the internet, many of which share the same general set of movies. Grab some popcorn and a healthy suspension of disbelief and slog through a few of them.

Unfortunately, there is some element of truth to this. There are innumerable attackers out there leveling both manual and automated attacks at our networks during all hours of the day. Some of them may indeed be the sugar-and-caffeine-fueled hacker nerds of movie fame, but some of them are also political activists, representatives of organized crime, members of foreign government–backed groups, spammers, scammers, and all manner of other unsavory types. Some of these groups have individuals working of their efforts full time, and with areas like cybercrime they could have up to 15 years of industry experience.

External attacks are typically driven by one of a few things:

- Wrath—Attacks carried out in anger or as revenge for some slight
- Greed—Attacks carried out for some material gain
- Glory—Attacks carried out for the purpose of later boasting or street cred
- Reconnaissance—Attacks carried out for the purpose of collecting information

Many of the media-worthy attacks that we see today are done in the name of greed. Breaches among the industries that handle credit card data have become rampant, with the resulting financial data being put up for sale behind (virtual) closed doors. Although this will, of course, vary by industry, a large portion of attacks on public sector businesses will fall into the category. Fortunately, this does lend some level of specificity to the types of attacks and defenses that we need to put in place as protective measures.

Internal Threats

In addition to worrying about innumerable attacks from external organizations, we also need to be concerned with those that come from within. According to the 20115 Verizon Data Breach Report https://paperpile.com/c/cTAM8E/oGnR [4], 20.6% of all security incidents and 10.6% of all confirmed data breaches are sourced from insiders.

Although this may not seem to be a huge number of insider attacks, consider that just a single attack could cause the breach that landed a company a great deal of negative media attention, financial repercussions, reputational impacts, loss of stock share price, and a great many other undesirable such impacts. In addition, attacks from insiders have the potential to be much worse than those that are external. Although external attackers have to do some measure of work to get to their target, insiders may literally stroll right through all of an organization's carefully planned defenses and back out again with the crown jewels on a thumb drive.

As security professionals, we need to have plans in place for how we will respond to an attack coming from a trusted source. As good example of this is the 2008 internal attack on the City of San Francisco computer networks https://paperpile.com/c/cTAM8E/JfW3 [5]. In this case, a disgruntled worker changed all of the administrator passwords for the network infrastructure devices and refused to give them to anyone else. Although this is not an attack in the traditional sense, it certainly crippled the ability of the organization to manage its networks and had the potential to have led to a much worse set of circumstances, had some network catastrophe taken place while the legitimate administrators of the network were locked out of their own devices.

In this particular case, the motivation was not malice, but indeed an overzealous desire to protect what Childs considered to be "his" network. The motivations behind insider attacks may not always be as clear cut and clean as those seen in external attacks.

Regulatory Risks

In addition to external and internal threats, there are a number of risks brought about by the regulatory environments within which most organizations operate, an area to which we will return in Chapter 2. For example, it would not be unusual for a company to be bound by regulations covering customer data, employee data, health care data, corporate reporting, sales records, and financial records, all simultaneously applied and all with a similar, but slightly different set of requirements. Even for large corporations with equally large budgets and staff, this can be a very cumbersome set of rules to follow and presents a large risk to the organization. Failure to comply in these areas can bring with it stiff financial penalties and can often affect the ability of the organization to operate in its industry. Large financial losses and loss of ability to conduct business are some of the main factors that cause the other threat vectors to be considered as threats.

Although we might be perfectly justified in discussing this as a risk management issue, it is such a large and prevalent problem that it also fits well here. This is not cleanly an insider threat. Although we could look at it that way, the enforcement and auditing that such a regulatory environment brings with it is carried out by external parties. To borrow a phrase from the bible, "out of us they went forth, but they were not of us" https://paperpile.com/c/cTAM8E/YUy6 [6].

We could look at this as an external threat equally as well; after all, this is a situation forced on us by external parties, but this is not quite right either. The regulatory environment exists to set the guard rails for our industry, to prevent those not blessed with an overabundance of scruples from engaging in unfair or unsavory business practices (this is only partially successful), and to protect consumers using the goods and services in question. We do want regulations to exist, but we must also be wary of the consequences of them being in place.

BENEFITS OF A FORMAL SECURITY PROGRAM

Given all of this, we need some method of dealing with all of these security-related issues. We need a formal structure or framework within which we can address the issues that we discussed earlier in the chapter to enable us to protect our assets while staying on the proper side of legal and compliance issues. A formal security program can help us to ensure the security of our information assets and provide a framework for security to codify our desired security level, help assess and mitigate risk, and help keep our program and practices up to date.

Ensure Security of Information Assets

One of the chief reasons to develop a formal information security program, if not **the reason**, is to ensure the security of information assets. In the risk assessment process that we have been looking at, this is largely driven by the system characterization portion of the risk assessment.

- System characterization
- Threat identification

- Vulnerability identification
- Control analysis
- Likelihood determination
- Impact analysis
- Risk determination
- Control recommendations
- Results documentation

Cataloging Assets

Among the outputs of the system characterization step will be a list of the assets involved, a summary of what the system does, and an assessment of the criticality and sensitivity of the system and the data that it handles. Among these items, the list of assets is, quite possibly, the most critical.

> **WARNING**
>
> It is absolutely vital when developing a formal information security program to have an up-to-date and regularly updated list of assets as early as possible. We cannot protect the assets that we do not know about. One of the hardest tasks down the road is to go back and retrofit an asset inventory. Once the process of building and deploying systems has begun and the task of maintaining an asset inventory is not included as an integral part, going back to bolt it on later will be detrimental to the security program.

Without some clear idea of what we are protecting, the task of protecting it becomes exceedingly difficult. The asset inventory should include, at a minimum, the list of systems and the criticality of each of them. This can later be used as the basis for conducting risk assessments, disaster recovery, incident response, vulnerability scanning, patching, and a host of other information security and information technology processes.

Classifying Assets

In addition to developing an asset inventory so that we know specifically what we are protecting, in the sense of individual hosts, it is also vital that we know what the importance of the individual hosts is. We might choose any number of factors to rate the importance of a given host, but a few of the more likely are items such as whether the host is internet facing or not, whether it represents a single point of failure, whether it supports a critical process for the organization, and whether it stores or processes sensitive data. There will, of course, be any number of factors that may be more or less important in any given environment, and we should choose those appropriate for our needs.

We can generally assign a criticality level to the system and can base further efforts in the direction of security it on this rating. As with the asset list that we just discussed, having a formal definition of the criticality of any given system is a foundational part of developing the security program. If we cannot say that system X is more, less, or equally as important that systems Y and Z, then we have no basis for prioritizing work toward securing these systems, incident response efforts, disaster recovery, and so on.

Provide a Framework for Security

A security program provides us with a framework in which we can approach the security for our organization and assets. Without a formal plan, our results are likely to be sporadic and vary greatly as one person or another who is involved in the effort applies his/her own interpretation on what the desired result and path to get there actually is. Where a formal security program gives us the equivalent of a GPS-based set of directions and a dynamically updating map on how to get there from where we are now, the lack of such a plan gives us directions relayed via the telephone by someone who is not clear on where we are starting from.

Codifies the Desired Security Level

A security program clearly defines the desired level of security for our organization. This will vary greatly from one organization to the next and will greatly depend on the information assets in question.

At a high level, we can look to our policies to define the desired level of security. Our security policy should define the rules that are in place to protect the information assets of the organization, including things like customer data, intellectual property, and so on. The security policy should set the baseline of the state of security within the organization.

The distance between the desired security level and the actual security level will be informed by the output of our risk assessment, in particular the control recommendations. These recommendations, based on the information from the rest of the assessment, should identify the areas in which there are gaps between the present level of security and the desired level.

- System characterization
- Threat identification
- Vulnerability identification
- Control analysis
- Likelihood determination
- Impact analysis
- Risk determination
- **Control recommendations**
- Results documentation

Provides a Mechanism to Assess Risk

Having a properly developed security program can help us to assess the risks that we might face as an organization. The process of defining the program will generate a risk assessment and the results of such will give us the material and information from which to build the program. This information will come from the threat and vulnerability identification, analysis of existing controls, determination of likelihood and impact, and the overall determination of risk.

- System characterization
- **Threat identification**
- **Vulnerability identification**
- **Control analysis**
- **Likelihood determination**
- **Impact analysis**
- **Risk determination**
- Control recommendations
- Results documentation

Given these items, and the resulting documentation from the assessment, the risks to the organization should be readily apparent. One of the very useful side effects of developing a risk-based security program is the output of performing the risk assessment as a part of the process.

Helps Mitigate Risk

Having a properly developed security program will also help us to mitigate both the present risks that we have uncovered and those that may be discovered in the future. The risk determination and control recommendations that are output from the risk assessment will directly help to mitigate risks.

- System characterization
- Threat identification
- Vulnerability identification
- Control analysis
- Likelihood determination
- Impact analysis
- **Risk determination**
- **Control recommendations**
- Results documentation

Although the risks and recommendations should be clearly defined as a result of the assessment, they will only help to mitigate the risks by providing a list of what needs to be fixed. The actual work of remediating the risks may be considerably more difficult than simply constructing a list of problem areas.

Often mitigation of risk will involve working with teams outside of information security or even outside of information technology entirely, and may be a very involved process.

Helps Keep Program and Practices Up To Date

Having a formal security program can also help to keep your security program and its related practices up to date. Most processes that we will define as part of the information security program, for example, the risk assessment methodology that we have been discussing, are iterative and cyclical in nature—when we get to the last step of the process, we return to the first step and start all over again, hopefully continuing to refine and improve the program with each iteration of the process.

As we build each portion of the program, we define what the iterations will consist of and at what interval they will take place. For example, we might decide that the security policy that provides the basis for the program needs to be reviewed at a minimum of 6 month intervals—every 6 months we take it out, dust it off, and make changes based on our last 6 months of experiences with implementing the policy, significant changes that have been made within the environment since we last reviewed it, and so on. We will also, of course, make updates to it as need arises, given some glaring fault that was pointed out or radical change that occurred.

ACTIONS

Enable the Business

Understand the role of security in the business

- It is of critical importance that we understand the role of security in the business. Security exists to enable the business to carry out its mission in a safe and secure manner. Security does not exist for its own sake. All of our decisions regarding the function of security within the organization need to be made with this concept in mind.

Establish context

- As a corollary to understanding the role of security in the business, we need to establish the proper business context for security investments and efforts to the stakeholders in the business. In many cases, security is seen as a cost or a tax on the business. It is very important that we communicate in terms that are relatable to business efforts.

Relate security investments

- Security investments should relate directly to supporting the business. They should protect our customers, enable now business opportunities enable gains in efficiency and reduce the effort needed to complete tasks, and be of benefit to the business. Security investments do not exist for their own sake.

Communicate risk clearly

- If we are having difficulty in gaining management support, funding, or resources to support security efforts, it is because we have not adequately communicated the risk of not doing so. We need to clearly communicate risk in terms that directly relate to impacts to our ability to conduct business.

Ensure the Security of Information Assets

Mitigate risk to acceptable levels

- One of our key tasks is to mitigate risk to the point of being acceptable. We will not be able to eliminate risk entirely, and it would be a very costly exercise to attempt to do so. We need to reduce the risks to our confidentiality, integrity, and availability to levels that we can live with. These levels will vary by organization.

Influence in a positive direction

- We should strive to continuously and positively influence the behavior of our organization in secure directions. Information security should not say no to anyone, but should give a qualified yes to those who consult us regarding their efforts. Becoming the security organization that always says no to its customers will result in security simply being ignored and bypassed as the business works to complete its primary mission.

Make security a top concern

- Security should be one of the top concerns in our organization. It should be reflected in every aspect of the business, and should be a core tenet behind the design and development of every technologically oriented step that the various components of our organization take.

Provide a Framework for Security

Establish policies

- Our security policies establish our risk posture and how we will manage it. The security policy defines what we mean when we say secure and provides the foundation on which to build the rest of our security program.

Establish standards

- Our security standards define how we will keep our information assets secure. They are the framework by which we manage the security of our intellectual property and the various data on which our business operates.

Make use of existing information security standards

- Following the adage of standing on the shoulders of giants, we should make use of existing industry-recognized security standards such as the various NIST special publications that relate to information security and the ISO 27000 family of standards, which covers information security systems management.

References

[1] Target data breach – Krebs on Security [Internet]. Available: http://krebsonsecurity.com/tag/target-data-breach/.

[2] NIST. NIST special publication 800-30 risk management guide for information technology systems. 2012. http://paperpile.com/b/cTAM8E/QWeV.

[3] Weise E. Eight all-time great hacking movies. In: USA Today [Internet], vol. 14. January 2015. Available: http://www.usatoday.com/story/tech/2015/01/14/hacking-movies-list-cyber-blackhat/21713327/.

[4] 2015 Data Breach Investigations Report (DBIR). In: Verizon Enterprise Solutions [Internet]. Available: http://www.verizonenterprise.com/DBIR/2015/.

[5] Sorting out the facts in the Terry Childs case. In: CIO [Internet]. Available: http://www.cio.com.au/article/255165/sorting_facts_terry_childs_case/.

[6] Nelson T. Holy Bible, New King James Version (NKJV). Thomas Nelson Inc.; 2009. http://paperpile.com/b/cTAM8E/YUy6.

CHAPTER 1

Develop an Information Security Strategy

INFORMATION IN THIS CHAPTER:

- Information security strategic planning principles
- Information security organizational vision and mission statements
- Setting the context through describing the information security environment
- Delivering the Information Security Strategic Plan
- Stakeholder engagement in information security strategic planning

Strategy is the plan for achieving an organization's business, mission, and objectives. In today's dynamic and rapidly shifting technological environment, strategic planning has been deemphasized and often criticized as to be no longer relevant. At the pace of technology adoption, planning from a strategy perspective has become an annual exercise rather than a disciplined formulation of near to long-term action planning along a defined three to five planning horizon.

Perhaps such long-range planning is no longer practical for those companies that heavily depend on technology, or are influenced by rapid changes in the market, but strategic planning still remains an essential part of defining clear objectives for the organization. Irrespective of the planning horizon, strategic planning defines clear business objectives, the respective goals to reach those objectives, strengths and weaknesses that act as tailwinds or headwinds, the key actions necessary to capitalize on these strengths or close critical gaps, and roles and responsibilities of those who are empowered to execute the actions to achieve the plan.

INFORMATION SECURITY STRATEGIC PLANNING PRINCIPLES

Business strategy is generally created at the upper levels of an organization, depending on the size and market focus of the company. Companies with a singular market focus and defined set of products or services may have a very

23

Building a Practical Information Security Program. http://dx.doi.org/10.1016/B978-0-12-802042-5.00002-0

narrowly focused strategic plan. Large corporations that participate in multiple markets with numerous products or services may have several business segment strategic plans that then roll up to a high-level corporate strategic plan. In either case, the degree of detail, specificity, and format is largely subjective. Some organizations have detailed documents that are very descriptive and lengthy; others may simply use a set of five or six presentation slides.

Creating an information security strategy and strategic plan is not any different from the planning process for the business. A clear and concise information security strategic plan allows business leadership, information security executives, information security managers, and their staff to understand what is the vision, mission, objectives, and plan for the organization and their role in its fulfillment. This provides the foundation of what is the direction and desired end state from "top down." The additional benefit is that the strategic plan creates the annualized organizational goals that are further flowed down to the individual employee, providing traceability in performance goal planning at the organizational and individual levels. A discussion of performance planning and metrics will be covered later in Chapter 10.

DEVELOP THE ORGANIZATIONAL VISION AND MISSION STATEMENTS

A vision statement declares the objectives of the organization. Often an internal statement, a clear and concise vision communicates the organizational goals to management and staff. The vision statement should paint the picture of what leadership believes is the ideal state or value that it delivers to the business. Vision statements define what the leadership wants the business to become, in terms of market focus, growth, values, or contributions to society.

The vision statement for an information security organization should lay out the goals at a high level and should support or enable the business leadership's vision statement. A vision statement can be also reflective of the organizational culture. For example, if innovation is a goal of the overall business, the information security vision should in some way support that goal. If lacking a higher-level business vision statement, the information security leadership should still attempt to relate the information security organizational vision statement back to the overall business's objectives and goals. An example of an information security organization's vision statement is provided.

> Information security will provide world-class, innovative, value-added solutions and services to our company; create a work environment where our employees are proud to work, and make a positive impact on our community.

Vision statements and mission statements are very different. Mission statements define the organization's purpose. These statements explain why information security exists as an organization or function. Similar to vision statements, mission statements should be short, clear, and powerful. An example mission statement is provided as follows.

> Through cost effective and innovative solutions, our mission is to educate and empower our employees to make informed risk-based decisions, work securely and safely, and reduce the technology risks associated with our business.

Ensure that the vision and mission statements are short, concise, clear, focused and even inspiring. Long, complex vision and mission statements tend to be "everything and the kitchen sink," which may not be reasonable or even attainable. They should be easy on the tongue and natural. They should be easy to memorize for both managers and staff who are all ambassadors of the information security organization back to the business. Lastly, vision and mission statements should be revaluated as the business changes; information security strategy can quickly become stale and irrelevant if it does not reflect the changes in business strategy.

DESCRIBE THE INFORMATION SECURITY ENVIRONMENT

To formulate the strategy and plan, the information security leadership needs to understand the environment that surrounds the business with a focus on its mission and goals. The information security strategy and strategic plan are based on the higher-order, strategic influences that create the function for protecting the business. Businesses generate their understanding of the environment and formulate strategies based on this understanding using several techniques, methods, or tools.

- Strengths-weaknesses-opportunities-threats or SWOT analysis
- Threat-opportunities-weaknesses-strengths or TOWS analysis
- Political-economic-social-technological or PEST analysis
- Porter's five factors
- Critical success factors

Originated by Albert Humphrey in the 1960s for Stanford Research Institute, the SWOT analysis is a well-known method of strategic planning. A SWOT analysis can also be a method for understanding the security environment or posture through the lens of internal strengths and weaknesses, as well as external opportunities and potential threat. The use of an information security aligned SWOT analysis supports the business strategy by addressing information security factors, issues, and challenges unique to the business and therefore complements the overall business strategy.

- Strengths—the most effective information security factors of the business
- Weaknesses—challenges, shortfalls, or gaps in the information security program

- Opportunities—factors that can help the company improve its information security
- Threats—man-made or natural factors that may exploit company information security weaknesses

An application of a SWOT analysis is provided—the management of an imaginary professional services firm that advises companies on financial services needs to start its information security program. The firm has 100 consultants and associates that either work from home or travel to customer locations to perform these services nationwide. The company employees are highly reliant on three core IT services—office productivity, collaboration, and human resources applications, which are offered as cloud-hosted Software as a Service. The company uses a Bring Your Own Device approach to end computing. The new information security leader is developing a company strategy using a SWOT analysis. After the security leader's analysis, a SWOT-based list of current information security factors is developed as in Fig. 1.1.

Strengths	Weaknesses
• New security leader is highly experienced • Strong company culture on being compliant with policies • Employees are generally IT savvy • Cloud providers have solid security technologies and practices	• Lack of security policies on handling company information • Lack of security awareness program • Employees are buying a wide variety of laptops and cell phones • No cloud provider contract clauses to report security incidents
Opportunities	**Threats**
• Cloud provider has additional services for protecting customer data • Discounted endpoint protection software available for all BYOD devices • Security training that can be bought "off the shelf" will meet company needs	• Regulatory requirements for financial data protection • Financial services are targeted by advanced, sophisticated threats • Cloud providers are regionally located in an earthquake zone • Lack of supply of experienced information security staff

FIGURE 1.1

Basic SWOT analysis quadrant.

For Strengths, the information security leader lists the most effective information security characteristics, for example, experienced security leadership, strong security practices in their cloud providers, and, since financial community is highly regulated in information security, a very compliance-focused culture. These strengths would be capitalized upon in the strategy development. In evaluating information security Weaknesses, the security leader noted that their employees are buying a wide variety of laptops and cell phones without any guidance on minimum features, such as security software, e.g., antivirus. Also there were no formal policies on handling company information on personal devices or security awareness program informing them of any policies or restrictions. Lastly, a weakness in the contractual relationship between the cloud provider and the company exists when and to whom security incidents are reported. These factors should be improved.

Opportunities identified in our exemplar by the security leader are factors—generally external, but can be internal—that can help the company improve its security. In our example, these may be security training and awareness products that can be bought commercially, subscription to the cloud provider's additional data protection security services, and specially discounted end-point protection software for various device platforms. Threats are those factors that exploit the company's information security weaknesses, and are either of a man-made or natural environmental source. For instance, as a financial services firm, there are regulatory requirements in protecting customer financial data. Likewise, these companies are often targeted by the most motivated and sophisticated threat actors, unusual organized cyber criminals. Also, as experienced information security professionals are in high demand, the company may have a lack of experienced information security staff. Lastly, the threat of earthquakes is a natural environmental hazard in our example.

It is from the SWOT analysis that high-level strategic objectives emerge from our financial services professional advisory firm:

- Establish security function and policies,
- Provide a safe and secure employee experience, and
- Leverage cloud service provider security offerings.

Likewise, the process offers goals or actions in support of the strategy objectives for evaluation and prioritization:

- Create company security policies that are relevant for financial services professional,
- Contract for commercial "off-the-shelf" security training for the employees that build upon the new company security policies,
- Identify specialized information security search firm for recruiting key talent, when needed,

- Purchase a discounted suite of end-point protection tools that can be hosted and deployed from an antivirus software vendor,
- Negotiate additional cloud security protections that meet regulatory compliance in protecting customer data, as well as information security incident alerting process if company data have been compromised, and
- Contract with a global data recovery capability outside the region of the cloud provider's data centers.

Each strategic recommendation should be evaluated using different criteria, for example, relative cost of the strategy's operationalization, ease or difficultly of implementation, relative effectiveness of the strategy, i.e., does it completely or partially address a weakness or threat. Strategies may include actions or initiatives that can be implemented in the short term ("quick wins"), whereas others may require expanded investments in additional staff, technology, or processes over extended time. Companies do not have unlimited operating capital resources for new recommendations and security leaders will be asked to prioritize their list of alternate strategies; when developing the presentation it is best to be prepared for the discussion rather than be sent away for more information gathering and analysis.

Search out and team with the business leader who leads the organizational or business strategy development and planning function. This individual is critical to the information security leader's understanding of the overall business strategic planning process, as well as the techniques and methods used in the planning process. An additional benefit is that the business strategy individual may not have contemplated information security as an environmental factor or risk to attaining overall strategic objectives. This individual could very well champion information security in other forums and efforts.

DELIVERING THE INFORMATION SECURITY STRATEGIC PLAN

Up to this point, the information security leader has gained support from stakeholders, as well as feedback and/or redirection on mission, vision, and initial strategy, the core activity is to move from strategy to planning. There are various methods in action planning, the most commonly in information security being either threat-based planning or capability-based planning.

Threat-based planning is essentially the measures of countering potential state threat capabilities with the defensive countermeasures by focusing on potential threats, man-made or natural. Threat-based planning assumes the organization is at a high state of protection at all times. The core of threat-based planning are answers to the questions "who is the threat" and "what might they do." A list of threats are developed and scenarios are developed as the basis for further detailed planning on architecture, infrastructure, and individual defensive technologies (generally the combined people, process, and technology) to counter the threat.

The methods of threat-based planning for information security planning purposes were heavily drawn from US military strategic planning processes in the post-Cold War era and the methodology is preeminent when threats to US interests are easily recognized and contingency, then determine the amount of force needed to prevail in that scenario. This approach lends itself to dynamic and static modeling and provides a quantifiable rationale for the recommended force structure. This approach to strategic planning continued well into the 1990s, with some variation of flexibility and adaptability added as corollaries, but was fully forced into reexamination in the post 9/11 realities of an asymmetric threat (e.g., international, borderless terrorism).

In its application to information technology, threat-based planning took shape in the 1990s. An example of threat-based planning is threat modeling. Threat modeling is a method for optimizing information security by identifying objectives and vulnerabilities, and then defining countermeasures to prevent, or mitigate the effects of, threats. Threat modeling takes on a defender's perspective.

The concept of threat modeling through attack trees was introduced by Dr. Edward Amoroso in 1994.[1] Attack trees describe how an asset, or target, might be attacked through the use of diagrams. In 1999, Bruce Schneider further proposed the use of attack trees to model threats against technology. "If we can understand all the different ways in which a system can be attacked, we can likely design countermeasures to thwart those attacks."[2] This means that threats are examined and defensive measures are identified. Threat modeling could be correlated with an organization's security policy and risk management in a way that business executives can easily understand risk, regardless of their level of expertise. The benefit was for senior management, security specialists, network managers, and application developers to work collaboratively in the prioritization and mitigation of threats.

Challenges in threat modeling for large, organizational purposes began to emerge in the post-9/11 era where threats shifted, morphed, and adapted at a much more rapid speed than before. Simultaneously, multiple threats sources materialized where in the past a single large threat existed and was highly predictable. In the realm of information technology, the threats are numerous and diverse and rapidly change and evolve. The ability to address all threats, at

---

[1]Fundamentals of Computer Security. Upper Saddle River: Prentice Hall.
[2]Attack Trees, B. Schneier, Dr. Dobb's Journal, December 1999.

all times, becomes untenable from a resource capacity, scalability, and budget perspective. Threat modeling also requires highly specialized subject matter experts with in-depth knowledge of organizational risk from an architecture, infrastructure, and application security perspective, which itself proves to be a challenge finding qualified security professionals with these specialized credentials. The pervasiveness of information technology in every business process, now requiring infrastructure and systems, introduces and aggregates a significant number of threats and attack trees, all which need to be addressed and comprehended for program planning. Lastly, threat-based strategy can be costly for organizations to try to implement—to address all threats at all times, assumes that security will be at its highest spending levels all the time. This is not to discard threat-based planning and modeling; for small organizations that only depend on a smaller set of applications and single infrastructure, threat-based planning may be appropriate, if not desirable.

Enter capability-based planning. Capabilities-based planning is more appropriate when threats are unpredictable, dynamic, and multifaceted. These types of threats do not fit in a single attack tree, scenario-based analysis. Capability-based planning focuses on multiple threats and applies the appropriate mix of required capabilities.

A major challenge with capability-based planning is convincing senior leadership that information security has established the proper linkage between an uncertain future and the specific investments requested to establish the relevant capabilities. This is where risk management perspective can make the linkage more understandable.

INFORMATION SECURITY CAPABILITY ROAD MAP DEVELOPMENT

Information security leaders and practitioners need a framework for guiding the organization around its strategic plan. Road maps are a common approach to articulate that plan. An information security strategic road map is a time-based plan that defines where a business is, where it wants to go, and how to get it there. It is a visual illustration that organizes and presents information related to the strategic plan and future tactical plans. They are an effective communication tool for managers, and link strategic initiatives with business plans.

A road map describes a destination in terms of goals, timelines, and intermediate stops on the way. It shows practical steps necessary to get to the desired destination. It considers interdependencies among steps and anticipates alternative routes that help optimize resource allocation and minimize risks. The road map is designed to structure the communication between the information security organization, functional support, and various stakeholders in a manner that allows the information security entity to:

- Act strategically when making investment decisions and managing projects.
- Securing buy-in from business leadership that makes it easier to earn buy-in from business users.
- Negotiate more effectively with leaders or staff who request new projects or initiatives that require significant, nonoperating effort.

Road maps should include the following:

- A strategy statement based on the earlier business and information security strategic planning.
- A prioritized list of improvement opportunities. This is generated jointly by the business and IT and should be refreshed periodically.
- A timeline of the initiatives and projects that will occur over the next several years with approximate start and end dates, durations, and sizes.
- High-level justifications for each project. These should be robust for projects over the next 12 months and simpler statements for projects past the 12-month horizon.
- The estimated cost and duration for each project. This is specific and reasonably accurate for projects occurring over the next 12 months and can be vaguer for projects that go out farther than that. An owner for each project. This is the sponsoring executive or delegate directly overseeing the project. For projects in the next 12 months it should be the specific person and for projects beyond that it can be the owning executive.

It may involve a couple of rounds of iteration before it is finalized. Here it is important to note that the information security strategic plan as articulated as a road map is where the organization aspires to be in a couple of years and what it would look like when compared with the current state. Without the linkage to strategy, it may become a "to-do" list with loads of activities and timelines and individual names who are responsible for various activities. An example road map that addresses active cyber threats is represented in Fig. 1.2.

The information security leader can use the road map to facilitate investment discussions with the rest of the executive leadership. The leader will use the road map as a baseline when discussing new projects or priorities with executives. It will help the leadership understand how to balance investment and project priorities and provide a way to visualize trade-offs. The road map will help them anticipate resourcing needs, plan assignments, software and vendor selection, and costs ahead of time, and make it possible to start visioning and planning with the functional owners well in advance.

Current State	Year One	Year Two	Year Three	Future State
Information Sources • Basic threat info from MSSP and Internet summary sources	Threat Indicators • Conduct integrated sessions with security personnel to review threat indicators / metrics • Assess current threat metrics for inclusion in quarterly governance boards	Information Sources • Expand threat information from MSSP • Analysis on threat feeds (and augment as necessary) Threat Monitoring • Hire dedicated Cyber Threat Intelligence person • Begin proactive monitoring of threat indicators • Begin proactive identification of the company as a target	Information Sources • Add information sources from other sources as appropriate and available • Formal membership in an ISAC Threat Monitoring • Continue Threat Monitoring activity • Expand as needed, dependent on need	Information Sources • Threat info from MSSP • Threat Info from FBI and other DHS sources Threat Monitoring • Dedicated resources monitoring threat indicators on the Internet • Proactive identification of Xerox as a target Threat Indicators • Integrated view of various metrics • Periodic update to CISO and other security functions • Dissemination of alerts and critical information to Xerox Resources • Dedicated Cyber Threat Intelligence resources
Threat Monitoring • No proactive monitoring of threat indicators • No proactive identification of Xerox as a target Threat Indicators • Various metrics such as AV, IDS, and other alerts available, but not collected / reviewed Resources • No dedicated Cyber Threat Intelligence resources				

FIGURE 1.2
Cyber threat road map.

STAKEHOLDER ENGAGEMENT

Once the strategy has been formulated into high-level alternatives, it is beneficial to begin stakeholder engagement to test the assumptions and recommendations. Formulating and managing an information security strategy, particularly those that are enterprise-wide, is full of challenges. Stakeholder buy-in is extremely helpful to gain traction, achieve momentum, and realize success. Stakeholder engagement is also very helpful for establishing risk appetite during the description of any one strategy and its importance to reduce risk, either real or perceived. Key activities in stakeholder engagement are identifying the key stakeholder, engaging as soon as possible, receiving feedback and input, refining or refocusing strategic alternatives, and reinforcing strategy through continual communication.

Identifying the key stakeholder is the process of really understanding who the key actors are, what they are concerned about, and their relationship to the information security strategy and recommendations. Methods to identify stakeholder include a vertical, horizontal, and external scan of organizations, functions, and individual personalities that have a vested interest in the information security strategy and program.

A vertical scan may reach up to the highest echelon of the organization, including the senior leadership and even board of directors, to the individual employee. A horizontal scan includes the operational entities and supporting functions of the business. Operational entities, or those lines of business that are customer facing, are important to engage as they are directly affected by the information security program as they go to market. Conflicts or misalignments that may occur from information security initiatives should be understood before they impact those business processes or delivery from generating revenue. Failure to do so will incur the perception of information security inhibiting the business.

Horizontal scanning involves the identification of other functional organizations that support the business. Functional entities, such as human resources, legal, communications, procurement, and finance, have an influence on the information security program as supporters of strategic initiatives as well as the avenue in which these program elements are delivered. An example is human resources (HR)—not only is HR an important function in supporting security workforce management program (i.e., recruiting, hiring, and retaining an information security professional), but also the HR team may additionally deliver information security training and awareness as an employee learning and development activity.

Once stakeholder engagement has been accomplished, the information security leadership can process feedback back into the overall strategy. Adjustments and tuning not only help refine the strategy to make it more appropriate for fit, but also help garner support from stakeholders as they recognize these adjustments based on their feedback.

SUMMARY

Information security strategic planning is about setting the vision, establishing short- and long-term goals, providing directions, and acknowledging the limitations and constraints that will guide the attainment of these goals. A clear and concise information security strategic plan allows senior leadership, executive management, and key staff to understand where the organization is expected to go, focus their efforts in the right direction, and describe the end state once they have accomplished their goals. A holistic information security strategic plan can be more effective when a disciplined, rigorous approach toward planning and execution is adopted. The methods described in this chapter require the integration of people, process, and technology dimensions of information security while ensuring it is aligned with the business and supports the overarching business goals. The better the alignment and integration to strategic decision making, the more effective the information security program will be in targeting and achieving its own state goals and objectives.

ACTIONS

Develop the information security organizational vision and mission statements.

- Built upon the overall business vision and mission statements, the information security vision and mission statements should be short, concise, easy to understand in nontechnical terms. The use of technical terms and jargon may confuse the business leaders to its real value and business benefits.

Describe the current information security environment.

- The information security team should first describe the current environment and security posture as an assessment of the "As Is" state of security. This is the starting point for developing forward-looking strategic plan and later road maps. It is from where the journey starts.

Develop the strategic plan

- The strategic planning process should describe future state and pathway from current state to future state. There are a number of strategic planning tools that the information security team can use; most important is to use and adopt the same strategic planning tools as the business and IT planning tools to ensure a common framework and alignment with the business and IT. The use of radically different planning processes and tools may confuse business and IT leaders.

Deliver a plan of action through information security road maps.

- Information security road maps provide a calendarized view of tactical initiatives that support the strategic goals and objectives. Each road map node will eventually become a formal project or improvement activity to incrementally advance the organization toward the desired end state.

Engage key stakeholders to test for alignment and relevancy

- Key stakeholder should be identified and continually updated on the progress to plan. Their support, both near- and long term, will help communicate the importance and relevance of the plan to other business leaders. Their support will be critical to receive the necessary resources and budget to execute the plan.

CHAPTER 2

Integrate Security Into the Organization

INFORMATION IN THIS CHAPTER:

- Understand the organizational security culture
- Integrate information security into business processes
- Establish information security business relationship management

Now that the strategy and strategic plan is established, the security leader will need to gain adoption and embed information security into the business. Integration of security into the business organization and operations can be influenced through three dimensions: organizational culture, business process structure, and business operations.

UNDERSTAND THE ORGANIZATIONAL SECURITY CULTURE

The culture of an organization is basically its personality. It includes the goals, assumptions, beliefs, values, norms, behaviors, customs, rites, history, and dress of the people who work for the organization. It is what makes employees feel like they belong and what encourages them to work collectively to achieve organizational goals. A strong security culture is both a mindset and mode of operation. One that is integrated into day-to-day thinking and decision making can make for a near-impenetrable operation. Conversely, a security culture that is absent will foster uncertainty and, ultimately, lead to security incidents that the organization likely cannot afford to incur. It might be difficult to move an organization's culture in a different direction or to make major changes, but actually change is occurring all the time due to a variety of influences, internal and external to the organization.

An organization's culture is generally reflected in its mission or vision statement and explicitly stated core values. The core values spell out the organization's basic beliefs and passions, i.e., what the company stands for and what it values. The mission statement is created based on the core values. The core

35

Building a Practical Information Security Program. http://dx.doi.org/10.1016/B978-0-12-802042-5.00003-2

values and the mission statement are used to guide the organization when making strategic, and even ethical, decisions. There are organizations that include the terms "secure," "security" and "privacy" in their vision and/or mission statements, particularly those in highly regulated industries that require data security. However, inclusion of the words "privacy" or "information security" in an organization's list of core values does not guarantee that everyone in the organization will value them unless management demonstrates its commitment. Many organizations periodically review their mission statements and core values, to ensure they reflect the organization's guiding principles. Security executives should use that opportunity to convince top management that information security and privacy should be included among their organization's core values. Security executives can use these concerns, cite laws and regulations that punish noncompliance, emphasize the positive impact on employees and productivity, and point out the impression it will make on the organization's customers. This will have the effect of making security a priority for the top leaders in the organization.

Indeed, the strongest influence comes from the top leadership position, something security professionals can use to their advantage to encourage the change that is needed to achieve a more secure organization. Many organizations recognize the need to secure their data but do not know how to make it a priority throughout the organization. To this end, one recommendation is starting with identifying the benefits to the business leaders so that they realize the need for the change, then identifying the specific steps to be taken to implement the change (i.e., the information security program).[1]

Since the business context is already understood at the highest levels, it is important to now "sell information security" in the appropriate levels and with the most important partners. The natural start is with the stakeholders identified during the validation stage of testing the strategy's fit for purpose. However, it is often the next level of the lines of business operations that will have to adopt, directly or indirectly, the information security program. These stakeholders will most likely be supportive if the value of the program is correctly communicated. You can justify information security value by centering on four common aspects of the value proposition for information security: compliance, risk, revenue, and reputation.

Compliance is well understood by all businesses as the foundation of good management. The policies and standards usually come in two forms, external and internal. External regulations, legal statutes or industry mandates will influence the security policies as a set of requirements that the business must adopt. Examples are statutory privacy requirements when handling

---

[1]Thornbury J. Creating a living culture: the challenges for business leaders. Corporate Governance 2003;3(2):68–79.

personal health information governed by the Health Insurance Portability and Accountability Act, national, regional, or even local legal statues may govern not only handling of personal identifiable information, but data breach disclosure requirements, and industry standards such as Payment Card Industry Data Security Standards outline privacy requirements and technical standards associated with credit card transitions. Internal policies will generally have the same weight of external policies. Internal policies may be an interpretation or foundation from the external regulatory or industry standards that govern the business. In other cases, internal policies are the statement of requirements—operational or technical—that must be adhered to for the proper functioning of business processes or systems. The value of the information security program to avoid noncompliance and possible penalties can be quite attractive.

The second aspect, risk, is one that must be tailored to the stakeholder's perspective. Each business leader or personality may have a different perspective on risk and the language and concepts should be slightly adapted to fit the individual's framework. Simply explaining the numerous threats that the business is exposed to will not convince everyone of the particular value of the program, particularly if the company has survived without any trouble to date. C-suite executives care less about a particular virus or how many times the firewalls were probed for a particular port or protocol. Chief executive officers and board members will care about reputation risk, as described later. Chief financial officers care about financial risk; they will be much more interested in the cost to a financial risk model that ties the return on investment of the information security program (reduce current costs, reduce future costs, and reduce the financial risk to the business). Business line executives are much more interested in business risk across their portfolio than a single system or application; they look for risks to the entire portfolio of processes or systems could aggregate significant downside to their quarter or annual plan. For managers who rely on their business-related transactional applications, that may be more concerned over the confidentiality, availability, or integrity of information being processed than the latest threat tactic using malicious software against a particular vulnerability.

The connection of information security and revenue is hard to make, particularly as security is perceived as a function than as a generator of revenue. Information security's return on investment, or more appropriately "return on security investment," is difficult to calculate, but something that can be achieved, often in terms of cost avoidance or savings. A transactional system security incident can result in outages that subsequently impact the business of generating cash. The financial value of information security program in getting things back up and running quickly is something that actually can be financially appraised. In some industries, information security may be viewed as a competitive advantage and valued by customers who may articulate the selection of one business over another based on information security capability as a criterion. For example, those companies that follow ISO 27000 framework and formally audit their data centers, applications, or systems against this framework often offer these certifications as a discriminator and valued aspect of their service delivery against others. Likewise, products that are formally certified under ISO/IEC 15408 Common Criteria for Information Technology Security Evaluation (commonly referred to as Common Criteria), international standard (ISO/IEC 15408) are provided preference over those products that have not had their security model formally evaluated. For the US Federal government, Common Criteria is used as the basis for procurement decisions in analyzing alternatives.

The impact to a business's reputation is not necessarily a hard story to tell. In recent years, the media and newslines have reported that several high-profile businesses have had their reputations dented by security incidents. Technology, retail, and banking industry firms have had reported compromises and outages due to internal and external threats. It is worthwhile explaining that not just external threats can damage a business's brand, as many companies have suffered bad media due to the improper or errant use of system, as well as fraud and identity theft, by an internal user. These high-profile incidents are very useful for explaining the impact that security incidents can have on a company's reputation. If a business has spent decades building a solid brand, explaining just how quickly and easily reputations can be harmed is an acceptable manner to emphasize the value of information security. Executives and managers understand the value of brand and consequences of brand erosion.

Beyond business executives and managers' adoption of information security culture, it should be well understood as a set of day-to-day practices by the employees. It would be a mistake to target massive change of culture at the employee level, particularly those that are global in nature, so information security should focus on a common understanding of information security awareness and a standard set of employee practices. First, ensure that a common information security awareness training articulates the key information security policies in easy–to-understand language. It should reference the documented information security policy and where it can be found on the corporate intranet. The training should outline what steps the business has taken to maintain information security, protect information, and acceptable use of company resources (inclusive of information). Beyond the employee-level training, role-based targeted training is also a mechanism to change behavior. One example is manager information security training; managers need to understand not only their obligation to maintain information security, but also how to identify indicators of employee bad behavior and how to correct it. In another example of role-based training, if the business is concerned about deploying secure systems, an applications security training and secure coding may be a manner to reinforce positive behavior with the develop community.

At a common employee level, antiphishing training is an example of proactive training to test their behavior in protecting data against clever social engineering attacks. Training should be constant to ensure an enduring effect.

INTEGRATE INFORMATION SECURITY INTO BUSINESS PROCESSES

There is a distinct difference between a business function and a business process. There may literally be any number of functional organizations in an enterprise—human resources, finance, legal, sales, marketing, and communications to name but a few common business functions. Business processes are less numerous. Business processes are generally a set of repeated activities that produce something of value for the business, stakeholders, and customers. The business process represents a stream of activities, their inputs, and their results. Processes have names like product development, supply chain, order handling, distribution, logistics, and market development. Processes can pass through many different organizational business functions. For example, a new product may have been originally designed through the combined efforts of the research and development, engineering, and marketing functions, then passed through many of the business's other functions on its way to market and customer hands. Functions tend to reflect how a business is organized, whereas processes reflect how a business behaves.

In integrating information security practices, it is extremely important to understand information security issues in the context of business processes. From a process perspective, information flows between activities, people, functions, and organizations as a process component. Information, as an asset, may have a process owner who creates or originates the information. Information users, or stewards, carry out the process owner's requirements in their part of the process flow. Basic information protection requirements such as classification, authorization, authentication, and accountability that are imposed on the information in the process-based view that may not reflect a pure "systems view" due to the information flows between organizations and individuals. Nevertheless, they come closer to a true reflection of the business needs of protection throughout the process. Therefore information security is affected directly in real time through process arrangements, tools, and people in those activities that are process based.

This poses a challenge to the business process owner who will need assistance from information security. The business process owners will need the guidance and advices on translating the information security policy in a meaningful way to impose protection requirements end to end. Information security must also develop an understanding of the major processes in the organization. Information security will need to understand the business process architecture that defines the processes, interrelationships ("interprocesses"), and information that flow through the business to its suppliers, partners, and customers. It is also essential to educate the appropriate management and business process owners the value of implementing controls, such as enhancing predictability, stability, repetition, and overall quality. Information security should not be perceived as inhibiting or throttling the business process; information security should support the overall business process objectives without creating a bottleneck. A further benefit is the cost avoidance of reengineering processes or supporting technology for remediating failures that may or have led to security incidents. The cost of reengineering may be more than the insertion of information security well before the design and development of a solution, product, or service. By participating in the business process creation or reengineering process, information security can be embedded in the business processes as a value-add partner.

ESTABLISH INFORMATION SECURITY BUSINESS RELATIONSHIP MANAGEMENT

The third key point of integration is establishing a partnership with the business. The classic integration is the placement, or alignment, of an information security representative or officer with the business entity in a direct support role. An information security officer plays a critical role in informing, advising, and alerting the general management on matters relating to the enterprise information security policy and program. The duties of the information security officer are typically managerial; the information security officer may be a single representative of the enterprise program to the business or may direct a team of analysts, engineers, and operations staff that are in direct support to the business unit. Some of the key responsibilities of the information security officer are:

- Reviews internal processes, standards, guidelines, requirements, and practices, both at the enterprise and local levels
- Updates internal control structures and standard operating procedures
- Conducts annual reviews for security compliance
- Provides security impact assessments and feedback
- Identifies security training needs and completing training requirements
- Protects identifying information collected in accordance with policies
- Reports proven or suspected exposure or disclosure of personal information
- Supports communication of security information to the unit
- Provides input and feedback on current and future security standards and initiatives
- Reports unit concerns and considerations related to security

The challenge in this role is that information security officer is often considered a support or subordinate role. The information security officer is perceived as a technical expert in the domain information security, but less of an expert on the business itself with the knowledge and skills of an information security officer. On a positive note, the information security officer role and relationship with the business has been evolving along with the advent of business relationship management. Business relationship management and the business relationship manager role were introduced as a process in Information Technology Infrastructure Library (ITIL) 2011. Business relationship management is a formal approach to understanding, defining, and supporting strategic and tactical business activities. Business relationship management consists of knowledge, skills, and behaviors that promote a more synergistic relationship between a service organization (e.g., information security) and its business partners. Concepts and principles that surround business relationship management are described in Business Relationship Management chapter of ITIL Service Strategy book.

Applied to information security, business relationship management addresses a fundamental principal—to gain a better understanding of the business and information technology (IT), therefore reducing the barriers and providing better alignment between the information security function and the business. A mature information security to business model will ultimately support two key goals: a defined relationship where information security has a specified purpose and role with the business and a set of processes that make up the information security to business management relationship lifecycle.

An information security relationship manager (e.g., Business Information Security Officer or Business Information Risk Manager) is the information security liaison for each major business line-of-business or entity. The information security relationship manager should be familiar with the business processes and provides advice to ensure maximum value for business-related information security requirements. The information security relationship managers should possess domain knowledge of information security and business acumen. The key traits of successful information security relationship managers are strategic vision and structured thinking, knowledge of industry trends in business and technology, strong teamwork and interpersonal skills, and excellent presentation and communication skills. The information security relationship manager is a crucial link between the information security organization and business partner by acting as an orchestrator, connector, and facilitator. The information security relationship manager responsibilities include:

- Aligns business, IT, and information security for synergies
- Defines key strategies for the delivery of information security to the business

- Understands and communicates information security concerns
- Recognizes new technology trends and forecast future information security requirements
- Works with project managers to embed security into project phases
- Helps evaluate IT project objectives and analyzes new business initiative
- Works with information security executive's financials staff on IT budgets

The information security relationship manager should be equally familiar with other IT functions (e.g., infrastructure, applications), disciplines, and processes to ensure maximum value for business-related IT and information security requirements. The information security relationship manager will need to engage with other IT functions, such as:

- Enterprise architecture. Engagement with enterprise architecture will provide the function a greater understanding of information security technology and solutions, or develop a strategy to synergize the overall IT and information security road map for various lines of business. Portfolio Management. The information security relationship manager will help estimate and prioritize various initiatives or projects on which the business would want information security to work on.
- Project management office. The information security relationship manager can provide subject matter expert advice on key information security related risks that need to be addressed in the execution of a project (i.e., requirement phase, design phase, or preproduction).
- Security and infrastructure operations. The information security relationship manager will need to understand current state as well as any incidents.

With the advent of the business relationship management discipline, security executives should leverage this paradigm as a manner to understanding, defining, and supporting interbusiness activities. The business should see the information security relationship manager as a trusted partner. To develop this deeper relationship, the information security executive and senior information security relationship manager should identify the partners within scope of information security delivery. Typically, the partner would be the person who represents the business entity, but not necessarily limited to the partner alone. Other interested parties may include management, customers, shareholders, professional bodies, and suppliers. The information security executive appoints the information security relationship manager to the business partner. Named individuals should be responsible for managing the relationship. This individual should be at an appropriate level of seniority responsible for managing the relationship and accountable to the business partner for performance.

Once appointed, the information security relationship manager establishes engagement and communications with the business partner. The information security relationship manager must identify business partner needs and ensures that the information security function is able to meet these needs. One of the main purposes of business relationship management is to identify business partner demand in a business context, and translate it into a requirement for the information security function. The information security relationship manager must understand desired business outcomes. This must be explained in business terms, such as improvements in data protection, reducing cost of security incidents, and greater maturity of security process. It is important to identify the benefits as well as value realization.

The information security relationship manager will also define how business outcomes will be achieved. The information security relationship manager, along with the information security executive, will need to provide the traceability from the desired outcome to how it will be achieved. There needs to be an agreement between partners on what and how information security will be provided to meet these outcomes. Lastly, the information security relationship manager should monitor change and manage it. The information security relationship manager will need to manage change requirements, drive improvements, measure satisfaction, and deal with incidents and/or complaints. This involves not only reacting to incidents, but also being proactive in the management of the business partner's expectations.

Although information security executives are keen on engaging the business through their information security relationship managers to enhance the information security to business relationship, it is also important to evaluate and improve the value of the relationship. This can be measured in two dimensions: organizationally and individually. The information security function's organizational success should be continuously measured using the following criteria:

- The quality and number of information security solutions that were proposed to the business partner for supporting or growing the business top or bottom line. This can be measured both organizationally and individually.
- The degree to which the business partner is up to date on key information security initiatives. This can be demonstrated in feedback from the business partner to the information security executive. Typically this is measured individually, to the degree that the information security relationship manager is responsible for keeping the business partner informed.
- Business partner satisfaction surveys on the state of the relationship. This includes an average measured satisfaction for information security delivery.

SUMMARY

Ultimately, information security helps deliver business goals. Integration of security into the business organization and operations can be influenced through three dimensions: organizational culture, business process structure, and business operations. The importance of information security as an organizational capability is constantly growing due to the shift in the information security's role from an "order taker" to strategic business partner. Weaving organizational culture, business processes, and business relationship management as an to integration framework between information security and the business facilitates the adoption of the information security strategy, objectives and goals while creating a relationship with the business as an equal partner.

ACTIONS

Assess and align information security to the organization's culture.

- Identify the key elements of the organizational business model, structure, and culture. Align security as a "value add" in maintaining compliance to external and internal policies, regulations, and statues, as well managing information security risks to business disruption.

Embed information security into business processes.

- Blueprint the business processes and identify integration points in the business processes for information security to enhance the protection of data. Business processes that have information security as an attribute or component in their design and execution are less likely to fail and introduce risk to data leakage or loss.

Establish information security business relationship framework.

- Establish a business relationship management framework for information security and the business. Introduce the role of Business Information Security Officer or Business Information Risk Manager as an advisory and consulting function to assist the business to meet their information security objectives, goals, and requirements.

CHAPTER 3

Establish a Security Organization

- Key factors in determining the best organizational structure
- Roles and responsibilities within security
- Where security should report
- Relationships with external organizations and authorities
- Skills
- Actions

In constructing an information security organization, there are a number of items to be considered. For example:

- What are the key factors that determine how to build the organization?
- Who should security report to in executive leadership?
- Who has what responsibilities at each level of the security organization?
- How do we handle relationships with law enforcement, partners, and external organizations?

These and others are all very good questions and are, have been, and will continue to be argued over by almost teams tasked with assembling this type of organization.

KEY FACTORS IN DETERMINING THE ORGANIZATIONAL STRUCTURE

There are a number of key factors that need to be taken into account when trying to determine the best organizational structure for a given environment. We should be looking at the mission of the organization, the risk appetite of the business, the culture, the size of the business, the scope of responsibilities, and the budget that we have been given to work with. Other factors may exist, of course, depending on the environment, and some may not pertain to particular environments.

45

Building a Practical Information Security Program. http://dx.doi.org/10.1016/B978-0-12-802042-5.00004-4

Mission

The mission of the security organization is, perhaps, the primary driving factor in how we structure it. The mission for our security team drives almost everything about how we develop the program. Does the team exist to meet compliance requirements and nothing beyond this? Does the team exist with the sole purpose of protecting customer or proprietary data and keeping us out of the news? Does the team exist to keep hackers representing the interests of foreign governments from stealing state secrets from a set of highly classified computer systems?

Our mission is the information security equivalent of the old existential question 'why are we here?' Sorting out what exactly the mission of a security organization consists of can be a bit of a tricky proposition. In most cases, the answer will be that we need to keep the bad guys out of our systems so our information is not compromised, all the while making sure that we do not interfere with legitimate users in the process. Sorting out the particulars of what this means can be a valuable exercise and needs to be done with the input of the key stakeholders for the organization.

Risk Appetite

Risk appetite can very much influence our security organization. In very risk-averse organizations, we are likely to put in a great deal more controls to mitigate cyber risk. Although not entirely, some large portion of these controls are likely to be technical in nature, thus incurring more technical costs and requiring a larger organization to support and administer them.

In an organization with a larger risk appetite, likely due to having a less critical or smaller set of information assets to protect, or due to outsourcing the hosting and management of such assets, we can get by with a smaller security staff.

For example, if we are performing security duties for a company that provides patient management solutions for chiropractic clinics, we might see this go either way. If we develop the software and host it and the data for the clinics in our own data centers, we might have a very low risk appetite. We need to ensure that the software performs in a security manner, that the platform is available for the customer, that the data are secure where stored, that the data center is physically secure, and any of a number of other issues.

On the other hand, if we were the same purveyor of patient management software but did not develop the application ourselves and helped customers host it themselves in the cloud, then our risk appetite might be very different. We are not directly responsible for issues with the software, we are not hosting the data, and we do not need to worry directly about the security and availability of the data center. By transferring risk to the hosting provider, we have taken on a role of governance, not management, although we are still responsible for the capability, even though we do not directly own it. These two situations call for almost entirely different security organizational structures.

Culture

Company culture may be a large factor in developing a security organization. In a very authoritative culture, such as we might find in a government agency, we might need a very different organization than what we would find in a more open-minded and free-thinking organization, such as we might have in a company that developed free and open source software to give away for use in third-world countries.

In our example government agency, particularly if we were handling classified data, we might need a very large organization to run a large number of security tools. In this case, we might need to take very heavy handed measures to ensure that none of our classified data walked out the door on a flash drive or went out over the internet, and that no malware snuck into our very carefully segmented environment. We might also need to staff more heavily for investigations and compliance audits to ensure that we were following all of the rules laid down for us to safely and legally operate. For the most part, confidentiality is the big driver in this environment.

In our open source development organization, we might find an environment on the other extreme end of the spectrum. Here, we are more likely to find a number of users working from their homes and a smattering of all different kinds of equipment present, running every conceivable operating system. Developers are likely to be collaborating with people in other organizations, and the intellectual property (IP) that we are working with is made to be given away. Without IP to protect or customer data to carefully safeguard, here we have a rather different focus. In this environment, we would need to worry more about protecting the availability of the systems and integrity of the source code for the projects more than anything else. The end points and the servers that hold the code would be the focus here and would require a smaller staff and set of tools than what we discussed earlier.

Size

The size of the organization and the number of assets that need to be secured can be a big driver for the structure of the security organization.

In a very small organization with few assets, we are very likely to find a team in the single digits with a jack-of-all-trades mentality among its members. In such small teams, we often cannot afford to fund an entire person to maintain a single technology or process. We are much more likely to see the case of each person on the team having at least a passing familiarity with each area and a much greater dependence on vendor support organizations when the time comes for very heavy lifting or to solve difficult problems.

In a large organization with a correspondingly large number of assets, we will probably see a great deal of segmentation and stratification. One very common example of such segmentation is between security operations (often called just operations, or even ops) and the rest of information security. This is typically done to move the repeatable day-to-day tasks such as configuring access, updating antivirus or intrusion detection system definitions, and so on to a particular team. We may also see other functions split off into their own teams, such as compliance, vulnerability management and patching, engineering, architecture, security consulting, and incident response, just to name a few. Exactly what these divisions are will vary heavily from one organization to another, and often tends to happen organically and based on need and the skills available. We should put careful thought into size-based organizational structure changes, as making such changes rashly or hurriedly can be hard to recover from if they are wrong.

Budget

Budget can be a huge factor when determining organizational structure. If our budget dictates a miniscule security organization of a single person, the organizational structure may be a very straightforward single line reporting to management. In a very small or very new organization, this may be exactly what is needed. With a team on the small extreme end of the spectrum, costs are likely to be very low. Even if we choose to invest in training and appropriately equipping our very small security team, which would be wise, the expense should be very low. This must map back to other factors such as risk appetite.

TIP

Although a one-person security organization, or one staffed by volunteers or students, may seem ridiculous, it is important to remember that we should always structure and scale security to be appropriate to the organization and assets that we are protecting. If our organization is very small with an infrastructure entirely hosted in the cloud or in the case of open source software mentioned before, a single person may be appropriate to the risk.

On the other hand, if we have a budget reaching into the hundreds of millions, we will likely have a bit more structure to go along with it. With such a large budget, we might assume a larger mission, as discussed earlier, and a correspondingly complex organization. In this case, we might have a chief information security officer (CISO), one or more layers of senior directors and directors, another few layers of senior managers and managers, and perhaps a layer of team leads under the managers. All of these employees will cost a great deal to support, train, maintain office space for, and so on, so it is important to take these items into consideration when planning out such a large set of teams. Along with the personnel, we need to make sure that roles and responsibilities are clear and support integrated operations. Although someone like a Fortune 100 company could have a large staff, they must still strive to be effective and efficient.

WHERE SHOULD SECURITY REPORT?

In addition to the question of what the structure of the security organization should look like is the question of where the organization should report in the management structure. We might find security reporting through information technology (IT) or outside of it; through Operations; Governance, Risk, and Compliance (GRC); directly to a C-level security executive; or to any of a number of other places. The concern is, if security reports up through it, that they may not receive a fair share of resources. Additionally, if security reports through the chief executive officer (CEO) or chief financial officer (CFO), will these positions understand and contribute to the security vision? There is no clear industry standard and this often comes down to culture and relationships within the organization.

Inside or Outside of IT

A large question in sorting out where to place the reporting for the security organization is whether it should report up through someone like the chief information officer (CIO) in the IT chain or not. On the surface, this does make a certain amount of sense. Information security is largely a technology-oriented organization and works closely with IT to ensure that systems are built in a secure manner, patches are installed, vulnerabilities are compensated for, malware is discovered and cleaned, and a thousand other daily tasks. As the two functions are so closely paired, having them report through the same management can be very useful.

On the other hand, having the same reporting structure over both IT and information security can also bring with it a set of issues. In many cases, IT provides the platform for the business to be able to proffer its goods or services and is vital to conducting business. Additionally, although this is a somewhat myopic point of view, information security is often viewed as being obstructionist. Information security often insists on things being done a certain way to appropriately protect the information assets of the company. To those who are in a hurry or do not understand the need for security, this might seem heavy handed and unnecessary. Having these two viewpoints reporting to the same management can potentially lead to issues and might become a conflict of interest.

Another potential reason for having IT and information security report separately is for purposes of supporting segregation of duties. If we have the same set of personnel, or even the same team (this is very common in small organizations) fulfilling both roles, we have a segregation of duties issue. Having the same personnel build the systems and then subsequently evaluate the security of how well this was done is likely to lead to issues in the long run.

Operations

One potential very interesting area to have information security report is to operations through the role of the COO. As the COO is responsible for the daily operations of the company, this can lead to a much better alignment between information security and the objectives of the business. In many cases, we see information security butting heads with the business functions as they try to carry out their task of running the company, generally with the goal of making money for organizations in the civilian world. It can be very frustrating for the business attempting to carry out its mission to be forced to fight with information security over every little task that it tries to accomplish in the name of success.

Having security report to the COO means not only that the business may have an easier task in accomplishing its goal, but also that the management of the business may be a little more security focused that we might expect with other structures.

Governance, Risk, and Compliance

In some cases, we may see information security reporting through the GRC portion of the organization, usually through the role of the CRO, where such a position exists. Where in this mix information security might fall can vary from one structure to the next, with any of them being equally possible. This is much more likely to be the case in compliance-based organizations.

In most implementations, the GRC group is responsible for making sure that the overall parent organization is playing by the rules that have been set forth for it. This usually involves ensuring compliance with any of a number of requirements, audits, risk management, and so on. In short, GRC is the road that information security's rubber is meeting.

The GRC function can be a bit of a two-edged sword to have security reporting through. It can be very useful in the sense of having access to the resources and data that this organization usually houses, in the sense of knowing where the security issues are likely to be found. Being able to go straight to some of the problems or anticipate them when implementing security controls can save a considerable amount of time and can lead to a greater level of efficiency.

On the other hand, having information security report to the piece of the organization that has some level of responsibility for ensuring that the company is operating within regulatory boundaries can lead to the two functions struggling against each other to a certain extent. If the GRC function is very closely monitoring every activity of information security to ensure that it is carried out perfectly to specification and polished to a mirror shine, this may greatly slow down the rate at which projects and tasks are accomplished.

Direct Reporting

In recent years, it has become considerably more common for information security to have its own C-level executive to report to, who will report to the CEO of the company. This person, who may be referred to as the CSO or CISO, holds responsibility for the security of the organization and typically reports directly to the CEO.

In some cases we may see both a CSO and a CISO, with the CSO being in charge of security for the entire company, including physical security, product security, risk management, and any other security functions all rolling up to this position. In this case, the CISO might specifically be in charge of information security and not necessarily the other security functions.

There are, unfortunately, no hard or fast rules for the use of CSO or CISO, so we are equally likely to see either or both of them used interchangeably, or one by itself in either type of position. This reflects on the relative immaturity of information security as a function within organizations that these distinctions have not been codified.

There are certainly advantages to having the security organization report directly to its own management at the executive level. Such reporting can lead to better support for the security mission, as the CSO is directly focused on the security of the company and not on other tasks. This may also mean that security is not competing for funding or resources with other portions of the organization, at least not below the level of executive management. Additionally, this reporting structure can give security a more informed seat at the management table where decisions are being made about things that fall within its purview. In some cases, not having a security point of view at such discussions can lead to later issues in helping to protect the company.

Other Areas

In any given organization, we might find security reporting up through almost any path. As the formal structure of executive leadership will vary to a certain extent from one business to another, the location of security will likely vary as well.

A somewhat less common area for security to report through is the legal department. This does make a certain amount of sense as many issues that concern information security concern the legal department as well. If security is taking part in collecting information for a legal case, either in support of the prosecution or the defense, they will need to work very closely with legal. If an employee is being investigated for misconduct, if security questions are being asked by or of a third party that the company is planning to do business with, or any of a great number of other similar cases, security often ends up paired with someone from the legal team.

Another common set of reporting areas for security is to any of the other C-level executives, i.e., CFO, CTO, or any of a number of others. Whether this makes sense or not depends on the organization in question, but this is also very common.

Ability to Support Security

The most important issue, above and beyond the specific reporting structure of the security organization, is the ability to support the mission of information security. The particular area that security reports to may, and likely will, vary with industry, business focus, changes in management personnel, and a huge list of other factors. This determination will likely be made at the executive management level during the formation of the parent organization, or the formation of the security organization.

To be effective, the information security function needs strong support in executive management, appropriate funding, skilled personnel, and a clear security state goal and road map to get there. Although some reporting structures may be somewhat more or somewhat less of a help to getting things done, as long as security is able to be effective in its mission, any of the above-mentioned structures can be made to work.

RESPONSIBILITIES WITHIN SECURITY

Whether we are discussing areas that directly relate to information security, areas that make use of security, or those that are slated with governing how the security program runs, there are a number of segments of responsibility that govern the function. We may see these changes to a certain extent, influenced by the size and maturity of the organization, but we will generally find that the responsibility for management of the security function, risk, privacy, and data fit into the structure in some fashion.

Bigger Equals More Complex

As we discussed to a certain extent earlier in the chapter when talking about reporting structure, the bigger the organization is, the more complex its structure will necessarily be. What exactly "bigger" is may vary considerably, including staff, budget, network, or any of a number of factors. Although it might be easy to look at this statement in simple terms and make a snap decision about running our security organization with minimal management, we will quickly run up against reality. A given person can only manage a limited number of direct reports effectively—this number is traditionally set at five. This limit is typically referred to as "span of control."

> **NOTE**
>
> Span of control, and the idea that direct reports should be limited to five, is an idea that dates back to at least the time of Napoleon [1].

When leaders' span of control strays too far above five, they become much less effective due to lack of time to work on their tasks, and often end up working longer days. The number of management-level personnel, when reduced to math, should be somewhere nearing the total count of the organization divided by five. Although this may not apply to staffing in places like call centers, it is key when thinking about security analysts and engineers.

CISO/CSO/CIO/CFO/CEO—Relationships and Roles

The relationships between and among the various C-level executives that we might find in any given organization can be complex, but this is usually due

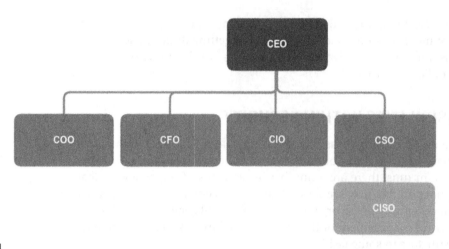

FIGURE 3.1

Typical C-level reporting structure. *CEO*, chief executive officer; *CFO*, chief financial officer; *CIO*, chief information officer; *CISO*, chief information security officer; *COO*, chief operating officer; *CSO*, chief security officer.

to creativity with the organizational structure. Given a CEO, COO, CFO, CIO, CSO, and CISO, we will likely see a reporting structure that looks something like Fig. 3.1.

In the structure shown here, all C-level executives report directly to the CEO, with the exception of the CISO, who reports up through the CSO. As we might expect, the responsibility of the functions is as follows:

- CEO—maintains overall responsibility for the organization
- COO—responsible for operations
- CFO—responsible for financial aspects of the organization
- CIO—responsible for informational aspects of the organization (typically IT)
- CSO—responsible for all aspects of security
- CISO—responsible for information security specifically

Information Security Committee

The information security committee, sometimes referred to as a security steering committee, is typically composed of management that has a direct responsibility for security and other key stakeholders. On such a committee, we might typically see the CISO and the management level below them, as well as representatives from other security-oriented teams such as IT, compliance, audit, risk, legal, privacy, CTO, and physical security. Next we will see members of the business that must accept the risk such as CFO, COO, lines of business owners, and sales. The makeup of the committee will vary heavily from one organization to another based on the reporting structure.

The information security committee typically reviews metrics that are derived from the day-to-day operation of the security program and discusses large security technology purchases and other such guidance for the security program. They can also serve as a source for helping to resolve issues and make decisions that need to be taken to a higher level of management.

Risk

In the information security world, management of risk is an area that can rest with a particular segment of the organization, often referred to as risk management, can be a responsibility divided among the organization, or can be a combination of these. Typically a security program will reach either a larger size or a greater level of maturity before a dedicated risk program begins to make sense.

The risk team, as we would expect, is responsible for addressing risk, as it pertains to information security. The primary vehicle of tracking risks and the remediation of them is the risk register, a concept that we will discuss at greater length in Chapter 5. The risk register provides us with a mechanism to document risks as they are discovered, rank them according to their level of risk to the overall organization, track their present status, and report all of this to the information security committee and the leadership of the information security organization. It is where we track risk acceptance and remediation decisions.

Privacy

Privacy is a segment that may or may not be a part of information security. Depending on how the reporting structure is assembled, we might see this report up through security, directly up through the office of the CIO, GRC, risk, or the legal department. The privacy team exists to ensure that the organization is compliant with regulations and legal requirements for the protection of the information that we are handling in the course of conducting our daily business. This might include customer data, employee data, or any of a number of other such items. Depending on the geographic area in which we are operating, there are a number of laws that cover how we protect these data, for example, the Health Insurance Portability and Accountability Act [2] in the United States, the European Convention on Human Rights [3] covering most of the European countries, and numerous others. Within the United States, each state has its own privacy laws.

Another, and unfortunately common, task that typically falls under the privacy organization is that of breach notifications. When a company suffers a breach that involves customer data, there are legal requirements for notifying customers whose data were involved in the breach in a timely manner.

WARNING

In the United States, the laws regarding breach notifications can vary heavily from one state to another. Companies that have suffered breaches may fall under the laws from multiple states depending on where they are headquartered, where they are operating from, and where their customers are located as well. It can be very important to consult legal counsel as soon as possible in the case of a breach to ensure that appropriate attention is paid to these issues. In the United States, the National Conference of State Legislatures maintains a list of breach notification laws by state [4].

Responsibility for Data

In addition to responsibility for the various components of the information security program and related functions, it is also important that we pay attention to the responsibility for the data on which our organizations function. From a data focus, we have data stewards, data owners, data custodians, and data users.

Data Steward

Data stewards are responsible for the overall management of the data and metadata that the organization is using. Typically, there will be a number of data stewards, each responsible for the data that pertains to a particular area, i.e., operations, IT, and security. Smaller organizations may only have a single data steward with responsibility for this effort across the entire company.

Data stewards will define the policies that govern the use of the data and metadata for which they are responsible and will also see to the implementation and execution of these policies. Additionally, they are responsible for making sure that the higher-level governance regarding the data and metadata under their responsibility is followed.

NOTE

Metadata is data about data. If we look at a text file that contains minutes from a meeting, the actual content of the file is the data. The file size, time stamps noting when the file was last accessed and updated, the author of the content, and any of a number of similar items, are the metadata. For any given file type, the metadata may vary. For example, our text file might not have much metadata at all, but an audio or video file may contain metadata regarding the frequency, frame rate, equipment that created the recording, applications on which the file was edited, and much more. Different regulations define metadata and if it requires protections. Some regulations define an IP address as personally identifiable information.

Data Custodian

Data custodians, sometimes also referred to as data managers, have direct control over granting access to the data for which they are responsible. They typically work directly with the data owners and data users to implement and manage access to the data and provide guidance and advice when new technologies or processes are being implemented that affect these functions.

Data custodians are often a part of the IT organization, sometimes operating as their own function within IT, or potentially as a part of another data focused team, such as database management or administration. Although this function does not generally report through information security, it is often responsible for ensuring that policies driven from information security are properly implemented and followed.

Data Owner

Data owners are directly responsible for the lifecycle of the data, i.e., their creation, use, and deletion when no longer needed. Data owners have the authority to grant or deny access to the data for which they are directly responsible, and also for ensuring the integrity of their data.

Additionally, data owners are key stakeholders in developing governance and the processes that implement it for their data. As the domain experts for the data in question, business owners should be the primary source of guidance on how the data should be used and maintained.

Data User

Data users are the customers of the data. Data users can be individuals or other organizations. The chief responsibility of the data users is to ensure that they store, process, and handle the data in a secure manner and work to maintain its integrity.

It is an unfortunate truth in the information security industry that users tend to be the weakest link in the security chain. There are many examples of users being careless with data and circumventing the carefully laid controls that were put in place to make sure that it was kept secure. Planning out user level security can be a complex endeavor from both administrative and technical levels.

RELATIONSHIPS WITH EXTERNAL ORGANIZATIONS AND AUTHORITIES

One important and often overlooked segment of the security organization is not really a part of the organization at all, to be technical about it. The outside organizations, agencies, vendors, and authorities with which we interact in the execution of our daily duties can be every bit as much a part and parcel of our success as those in our direct employ. In the course of our information security duties, we are likely to work with others in our chosen industry (both information security and the industry in which our parent organization operates), auditors, law enforcement at various levels, and a host of others.

Industry

Relationships with other organizations operating in the same industry as we are can be very helpful when carrying out our duties as security professionals, whether these relationships are in the security industry, the industry in which our organization operates (retail, utilities, etc.), or a combination of both.

Other Organizations in the Same Industry

Relationships with others who operate in the same industry as we do can be very helpful, as they can provide us with a large amount of data that is both security program specific and specific to an environment that is very likely to be similar to ours in many ways. Other programs that have been developed to operate in industries that are the same as ours have likely been developed to a similar set of standards, compliance requirements, and issues as our own. This can be very helpful when evaluating new technologies, working to remediate issues, putting new pieces of program in place, or developing them further, and a great number of similar areas. In particular, if we have the opportunity to develop contacts at similar organizations that have more mature or further developed information security programs, this may afford us the opportunity to be "standing on the shoulders of giants" [5] and learn from the lessons and mistakes of those who have been down the same path before us.

Another benefit to working with others operating in the same industry is that we may be able to work with others to afford us all some additional layer of security from shared knowledge. To borrow from Benjamin Franklin, "We must, indeed, all hang together, or most assuredly we shall all hang separately" [6]. We can see examples, for instance, in the retail industry, where a number of security breaches at large retailers bore a striking set of similarities in the types of attacks used, specific malware used, and internal patterns of infrastructure organization. Closer cooperation among these companies may have alerted those attacked later to some indicators to look for in their environments a little sooner than what occurred. The potential downside of such sharing is that it might result in security issues being publicly revealed before we are ready to do so ourselves.

Industry Bodies

Although informal cooperation among those working in the same or similar industries can be beneficial, so can formal cooperation in the same avenues. With this specific idea in mind, a number of Information Sharing and Analysis Centers (ISACs) exist across multiple industries for the express purpose of sharing information centering on particular industries. ISACs exist for utility companies, finance, retail, aviation, defense, IT, and a great number of others. These can be a treasure trove of information regarding industry-specific issues and can also provide a forum to discuss things in a safe environment and network with others of a similar focus. We will discuss ISACs to a greater extent in Chapter 5.

Auditors

Our relationships with auditors can be a bit of a two-edged sword. Auditors exist to point out where we are not compliant or not meeting standards, which is generally a poorly received message. Such audits, even when bearing news that is bad, or that we would rather not hear, can be of benefit to us in pointing out areas that we have opportunity for improvement. The worst sort of audit is the one that finds no problems for us to fix. This may mean that the auditor was not sufficiently thorough.

On the positive side, auditors can provide us with a list of areas in which we can improve our program and practices. This can be very helpful in making improvements as it gives us some specific directions for improvement and, hopefully, some specific recommendations. An item of particular importance in many environments is that audit findings will generally be reported to some level of management over the security program. Although we might think that this would be a negative thing, and in some cases there might be a certain amount of negativity associated with such things, audit findings do two things for us. First, they get management attention on specific items that we might have trouble remediating otherwise. Management focus on issues can get us help in working with other teams and holding people accountable for getting the problems rectified. Secondly, audit findings will often make getting funding to fix the issues a considerably easier task that we might otherwise have. Although there is a certain amount of weight attached to the security team asking for funds to fix a problem or enhance a technology, an audit finding is a different case entirely.

On the negative side, auditors have the potential to cause a great deal of trouble for the organization being audited. This does not always directly relate to issues that are found during the audit, although these have the potential to bite us if many such issues are found, but more often relates to the quality of the audit itself. If the audit is not performed diligently and to the set of standards upon which the organization should be working from, then the audit may be working against improving the program, not for it. For example, if we are working from the National Institute for Standards and Technology (NIST) standards for developing security programs and our auditors assess us against the International Organization for Standardization (ISO) (yes, this acronym is out of order from what we would expect) 27000 series of standards for security programs, we will end up with differences in expectation for what the program looks like.

Lastly, it can also be of benefit for us to switch auditors occasionally, whether these are internal or external parties carrying out the audit. There is, arguably, some benefit to having an auditor who is familiar with the environment being audited; however, this can also grow to be a negative over time. When we are very familiar with a particular thing, and this is not something specific to audits, we begin to develop preconceptions about what it should or does look like, and may gloss over differences between what we expect to be there and what is actually there. This can lead to audits that do not benefit us greatly due to there being gaps between issues, or lack thereof, and what the environment actually looks like.

Law Enforcement and Government

Contact with various law enforcement agencies can be critical to the success of the security function. Some organizations may end up in the position of needing to work with local law enforcement for issues that involve a local and/ or physical component, federal law enforcement for cybercrimes in general or for larger scale issues, and international law enforcement for issues that span the borders of multiple countries.

Local

Building relationships with local law enforcement can be of great importance when dealing with security issues that have a local focus or local component. One unfortunately all too common occurrence of such a case where local law enforcement can be of help is the clandestine placement or use of skimming devices. Skimmers are generally devices that are physically placed in environments where credit cards are in use to capture the track data from the card being swiped and potentially the Personal Identification Number used with the card as well. As such devices are often wired or inserted into the payment terminal, they require physical placement, thus a potential need for bringing in local law enforcement to investigate or deal with the attacker on a physical level.

NOTE

For more information on payment card skimmers, see the series by Brian Krebs on the subject [7]. There are a surprising number of ways that such devices are integrated into payment terminals in ways that are almost indistinguishable from the original equipment.

Federal

Federal law enforcement involvement is frequent where there are investigations of cybercrime. In most US-based cases, the agency involved will be the Federal Bureau of Investigation (FBI), or in some cases, depending on the exact nature of the crime, the Secret Service.

One of the services that the FBI provides is its flash alert service, often found to contain alerts pertaining to current or upcoming cyberattacks, malware, botnets, and other similar activity. These alerts will often contain Indicators of Compromise, such as filenames, hashes, IP addresses, domain names, and other information that we can use to search our own enterprises for signs that we have been a victim of the particular attack or method discussed in the alert.

Additionally, federal law enforcement may have visibility to outside data or signs that a particular organization has come under attack without the organization's own security measures being alerted. This is often information based on other ongoing investigations that the agency is working on, or data that they have collected as a result of observing such activity.

International

For issues that span the borders of multiple countries, we may need to recruit the assistance of international law enforcement agencies, or work with agencies from multiple countries cooperating internationally.

Cases involving international issues can be very complex indeed, as the laws governing the types of issues that we are likely to be concerned with can vary widely from one country to another. What might be a very serious crime and accompanied by a very stiff set of consequences in one country may be completely legal and of no consequence whatsoever in another. Additionally, the issue of correctly attributing the origin of the attack to a particular geographic location and host system can complicate such engagements even further.

For most organizations, any international portion of an investigation where law enforcement is involved will be conducted through agency based in our local country. This is generally a good thing, as these agencies are trained in and familiar with such tasks.

ACTIONS

Organizational

Develop organizational structure

- Determine what the overall organizational structure at the executive level looks like. For security purposes, this needs to be fleshed out enough to include the full chain of reporting for all the major security and IT functions.

Determine where security reports

- Determine where in the organizational structure security should report up through. This may vary widely from one organization to another and may change over time as the organization matures.

Define security roles and responsibilities

- Define the roles and responsibilities for information security from the lowest level of management to the CSO or executive that is fulfilling this function.

Staffing

Determine skill sets required to support capabilities

- Based on the security capabilities required, determine what skill sets are needed to carry them out. Depending on the size of the organization, these skill sets may be sourced in-house or contracted out.

Determine the number of staff required to support capabilities

- Determine how many staff are needed to support the required security capabilities. As with skill sets, the number of staff may or may not need to be augmented with contract personnel.

Align staffing with required capabilities

- For the required security capabilities, ensure that the staff being hired or present are capable of supporting them. This may mean making decisions about which capabilities are being supported internally and externally, and the degree to which specialized security skills, such as digital forensics or penetration testing will be developed in-house.

References

[1] Executive Oversight: What's the Optimum Number of Direct Reports? – Gary Keller, the millionaire real estate agent, KellerINK, mrea, span of control, presidential election, org charts, organizational model [Internet]. Available: http://www.kellerink.com/blog/executive-oversight-whats-optimum-number-direct-reports.

[2] OCR. Understanding health information privacy. U.S. Department of Health and Human Services. 2007. Available: http://www.hhs.gov.

[3] European Convention on Human Rights – Council of Europe [Internet]. Available: http://www.coe.int/en/web/human-rights-convention.

[4] National Conference of State Legislatures [Internet]. Available: http://www.ncsl.org/research/telecommunications-and-information-technology/security-breach-notification-laws.aspx.

[5] Phrase Finder is copyright Gary Martin 1996–2015 All Rights Reserved. Standing on the shoulders of giants – meaning and origin [Internet]. Available: http://www.phrases.org.uk/meanings/268025.html.

[6] Franklin's Contributions to the American Revolution as a Diplomat in France [Internet]. Available: http://www.ushistory.org/valleyforge/history/franklin.html.

[7] All About Skimmers — Krebs on Security [Internet]. Available: http://krebsonsecurity.com/all-about-skimmers.

CHAPTER 4

Why Information Security Policies?

INFORMATION IN THIS CHAPTER:

- Align information security policies to the organizational profile
- Types of information security policies
- Information security policy governance and management

The translation of the information security program's strategy and planning into organizational adoption is through the alignment of information security policy with the business goals. Any policy is an organizational statement of intent. Information systems security policies are designed to inform the members of an organization of their obligatory responsibilities for protecting the information systems of their organization. Policies are adopted by a company as a statement of purpose, objectives, and roles and responsibilities. They are formally promulgated by the concurrence of company leadership. An information security policy defines the objectives of the information security function and provides a high-level strategy toward achieving the stated objectives. An organization without business-aligned information security policies is likely to be a fragmented collection of standards, guidelines, and procedures that indiscriminately addresses a holistic practice of information security.

ALIGN INFORMATION SECURITY POLICIES TO THE ORGANIZATIONAL PROFILE

An information systems security policy and subordinate standards, guidelines, and procedures integrate the many different aspects of an enterprise information security program to achieve business objectives. An enforceable written policy helps ensure that everyone within the organization coherently behaves in an acceptable manner with respect to information security. Information security policies provide a framework for the business that can be followed by all employees. Policies will help to define and categorize information as an asset, inform the employees on their responsibilities to protect these important

63

Building a Practical Information Security Program. http://dx.doi.org/10.1016/B978-0-12-802042-5.00005-6

assets from unauthorized access, modification, disclosure, and destruction, and how to respond and report to policy violations.

Information security policies are also useful beyond the purpose of protecting company information assets. It is essential for companies to be able to demonstrate compliance with current regulations and legislation. Information security policies can assist the company in demonstrating its compliance requirements to regulatory, legal, and even contractual requirements. In many market industries, companies are required to show compliance with regulatory or legal frameworks that govern their participation in a particular industry or business process. Legal requirements surrounding Sarbanes Oxley (SOX), Gramm-Leach-Bliley Act, Payment Card Industry (PCI), and Health Insurance Accountability and Portability Act (HIPAA) require companies to have specific protection in place, which start from simple policy statements surrounding the requirement. Policy support compliance by mapping the policy to operational or technical standards, guidelines, and procedures to ensure the requisite controls are in place.

Policy is important in large complex enterprises to set expectations of all business entities and their associated information technology (IT) departments. It should reflect the generally accepted principles and best practices that should be adopted across geographic and organizational boundaries. This is particularly relevant where corporate culture toward security may not be uniform due to cultural difference and the need to set expectations of behavior that might not be inherent in these segments.

Policies can also introduce technology initiatives and drive more security-aligned technology adoption when those policies become translated into technical requirements. Policies can be the engine of change by outlining the secure deployment and implementation of emerging technology and its business use. For example, the introduction of a new cloud-based storage solution or Bring-Your-Own-Device initiative will require certain new behaviors with technology, and a support information security policy will drive the secure adoption through why and how adoption will be achieved. An effective security policy should fulfill many purposes. It should:

- define information as a company asset;
- underscore the importance of information as an asset;
- set the rules of behavior in handling the information asset;
- describe how to report a suspected policy violation;
- articulate the consequences of policy violations;
- authorize the investigation of policy violations.

TYPES OF INFORMATION SECURITY POLICIES

Policies are generally organized in a top-down hierarchy that is defined by the company's leadership for proper governance. An umbrella organizational policy is the highest statement of policy; any subordinate policies will be additional levels of granularity to the detailed configuration of specific technology, yet traceable to the higher level policy.

Organizational Policy

An organizational or institutional policy details the purpose, ownership, roles and responsibilities, and related documents or related policies. The organizational policy is often the highest level policy statement from which all other polices, standards, guidelines, or procedures draw their legitimacy. As a written policy, it should be mandatory and reflect management's requirements for organizational behavior. It should not be laced with language about a specific technology or vendor product, but agnostic to how the policy objective is met.

Standards

An information security standard describes the implementation and management of information security controls. A standard provides an information security control to meet required specifications, including those for meeting specific industries or regulatory compliance objectives. There are several well-recognized standards frameworks.

- The Control Objectives for Information and Related Technology (COBIT). COBIT is a framework developed in by the Information Systems Audit and Control Association (ISACA), an independent organization of IT governance professionals. COBIT originally focused on reducing technical risks in organizations, but has evolved with each successive version to include alignment of IT with business-strategic goals. It is the most commonly used framework to achieve compliance with SOX rules.
- The International Organization for Standardization (ISO) 27000 Information Security Management. The ISO 27000:2013 series provides a very robust information security framework for any industry. Rooted in the earlier British Standards Institution (BSI) Standard 17799, it is often referred to as the information security version of ISO 9000 quality standard. ISO 27000 is further decomposed into several substandards based on the content. For example, ISO 27000 provides a description of the standard, ISO 27001 defines the program requirements, and ISO 27,002 defines the operational information security program requirements.
- The National Institute of Standards and Technology (NIST) Special Publication 800. NIST SP 800 series provides general and specific guidance on nearly all aspects of information security. NIST SP 800-53 is model framework that US government agencies and suppliers use to comply with the Federal requirements. Even though it is specific to government agencies, the NIST framework could be applied in any

other industry and should not be overlooked by companies looking to build an information security program.

These frameworks also share multiple security or compliance objectives that are synergistic or allow the control to meet all frameworks' intent. For example, COBIT, ISO2002, and NIST 800-53 all define the necessity of a security policy; developing a security policy can fulfill multiple frameworks and standards if properly crosswalked and normalized to meet the common objective. This equally facilitates a "test once, comply many" audit or inspection process where the company needs to meet multiple legal or regulatory requirements due to its participation in multiple industries. There are several common standards that companies should evaluate as the basis for its standards framework.

Procedures

Procedures consist of step-by-step instructions to assist workers in implementing the various policies, standards, and guidelines. A procedure is the specific step-by-step instructions to properly operate a control or execute a process. A procedure could be a written instruction on how to configure auditing on a server, run a vulnerability scanner, or implement a firewall rule. A process may also be defined through the use of a desktop procedure, such as how to triage a security event. For procedures, the information security team has the option of not creating the procedures themselves, but adopting commonly recognized standard configurations. The benefit of using prepared standard configuration procedures or standards is that the effort to research test and document the procedure is borne by the originating authors. Secondly, these common configurations are template for use in automated configuration or compliance management tools to allow validation. The disadvantage is that, although standardized, the company's specific technology deployment may require deviations that need to be documented and accommodated. Some popular standardized configuration procedures are those developed by the National Security Agency Central Security Service, NIST, Center for Internet Security, and others.

Guidelines

Guidelines consist of recommendations that may support a policy or standard. Guidelines are related to information security best practices that support a policy or standard. For example, a policy may direct that employees must report security violations to a centralized mailbox or operations center's internal phone number. The supporting guidelines may be a list of important information that would support the report (i.e., when did it occur, who was involved, computers affected). For example, standard may dictate the use of encryption for sensitive information. The companion guideline may be what types of information should be encrypted.

Checklists

A checklist is used to validate or confirm certain conditions or configurations associated with the security policy or standard. The checklist is used, often by IT or security staff, to validate that a condition or configuration is correctly implemented. For example, a system administrator may use a checklist to set up logging for a server, set permissions, or assign rights. Each configuration is validated on the checklist as being properly set and secure. A second example is the use of checklist during inspections or assessments. The auditor will use the checklist to note conformance or nonconformance with a specific policy or checklist.

INFORMATION SECURITY POLICY GOVERNANCE AND MANAGEMENT

Information Security Policy Governance

Many organizations and companies have a policy management framework that defines the process of how to promulgate a corporate policy or standard. It defines the purpose of policy and policy types, describes how to determine and assign policy ownership, guidance on policy development, the process of submitting a policy for promulgation (adoption), the communication of policy to the organization, and the review process to ensure currency. In most companies, the policy management function is centrally managed by the corporate home office. It is important for the security leadership to understand the policy management process to effectively craft, submit, and manage their policy inventory. For general IT policies, some information management functions centrally manage all IT policies related to the delivery of IT to the company. Each IT organization—Application, Infrastructure, and Information Security— should take ownership of a set of relevant policy, standards, or procedures related to the delivery of its particular service area.

Information Security Policy Management

Policy management is a continuous cycle of development, publication, maintenance, and retirement. Companies require a well-defined and organized approach to manage the life cycle that ensures information security policies are created and approved.

Policy Development

It is critical to select who is going to be involved in the development phase as early as possible. Ideally, the team or individual who develops the policy should ideally also be the process or technology owner and responsible for setting expectations for policy enforcement once promulgated. For information security policies, it will most likely be the information security function.

The membership of the policy development team will vary depending on the scope, scale, and complexity of the policy topic or subject. For a policy that is narrow in scope and targeted toward a particular process, technology, or population, the policy development team may be small or a single individual. For those policies that are long reaching with large scope, a multifunctional policy development team may be more appropriate. The following roles should be involved:

- **Information Security Leader or Focal Point**. Since the information security policy is an information security initiative, it is expected that a leader or focal point be designated to manage the development phase up to final promulgation. Overall responsibility may be assigned to a key person with the other development team members in a supporting role. This focal point will guide each policy through development and subsequent revisions. Managing the development phase as a project, it is the focal point's responsibility to set the tasks, schedule, and resources necessary to successfully deliver the policy document.
- **Subject Matter Experts**. The policy development team will most likely be staffed by subject matter experts in the topic or subject of the policy. It is most likely that subject matter experts will be drawn from the information security team. In addition to the information security team, the policy development team may need the expertise of other IT staff who have specific technical knowledge in the subject domain. These experts should be familiar with the technology or process associated with the policy. They can provide good insight if the policy is actually reasonable, feasible, and enforceable.
- **Legal Counsel**. The Office of General Counsel, or similar function, should review the policy at a logical point of the development process, often as it approaches final draft. Legal counsel can provide advice on the policy applicability or conflict with any legal or regulatory statutes or rules. The privacy function often resides in the legal department and the privacy officer will need to review for any conflicts with privacy concerns. Lastly, the general counsel may provide input to the feasibility of enforcement if any policy violations occur.
- **Internal Controls and Audit**. The Internal Audit and Internal Controls departments should review the policy for consistency with the general control and audit framework (e.g., SOX) for the company. Internal controls department should be consulted on the coherence of the policy with other controls as a best practice. Internal audit will provide good feedback on the ability to monitor and audit the policy in terms of their audit procedures.
- **Human Resources**. Many information security policies are employee centric on what is and what is not acceptable behavior or use of

IT. Human Resources (HR) department may need to review the information security policy for coherence and consistency with other HR policies that are security-related. They will also examine the policy for the ability to enforce and what would be the general consequences for policy violations. The information security focal point or team should be able to communicate the gravity or impact of not adhering to the policy so as to determine if the violation may be considered ground for termination.

- **Technical Writer**. A technical writer can be useful in determining the appropriate structure, style, and format for the policy. Although some information security departments may have a technical writer in their group, more often than not, a technical writer will be sourced from a general pool of technical support staff as a shared resource. In even smaller companies, this resource may not be available and left to the information security team to both author and edit the draft policy. The technical writer can help organize the policy, edit the various drafts, and proofread the initial policy for spelling or grammar errors. An additional benefit is that, if the technical writer has experience writing company policies, he or she can jump-start the policy creation through their familiarity with style, as well as the process to get a policy at the level of acceptability that management is accustomed to. It is important to adopt the corporate style guide to make them publishable. If one exists, it should be used to ensure policies have the same look and feel as other corporate policies, avoid rewrites, and help them to be more quickly accepted as corporate documents.

- **Business Partner Representatives**. At a certain point of creating the policy, it is useful to test the policy for acceptability and receptiveness with a business representative. A business partner can provide feedback to the policy development team on issue such as language, prose, and style. Technical staff tend to talk in dry technical terms; the business representative can help the team adapt the intent and content in business terms that are more recognizable than technical jargon. If employees cannot understand the policy, they are less likely to follow it. Also, for global companies, a business representative from each region may be required to review the policy in the native language in which it is deployed. The team should not rely exclusively on contracted translation services, but use business representative to vet and even correct inaccurate translations. Where a current information security policy is being reviewed or updated, testing with a business representative helps determine the success of a policy's intent. This will help indicate whether an update or revision is required. This is particularly meaningful where policies have been in place for several years and in danger of becoming irrelevant.

Once the team is identified, the hard part of policy development is the drafting of the policy. There are three key considerations in the drafting of the policy: maintain the purpose and scope of the policy, identify the audience and ensure applicability, write the policy at the correct level or detail necessary, and identify any exception conditions and process for attaining an exception.

TIP

It is important to maintain the purpose and scope of the policy during its development. A policy does not create itself; there was a need or requirement, either based on operational need, to meet a regulatory requirement, or even threat-driven. The policy development team should constantly guard itself from dragging irrelevant side issues into the policy or attempt to cover multiple issues or reasons into a single policy. In either case, the danger is that the policy becomes unclear or obtuse; the reader may become confused exactly what the policy is attempting to address or what actions he or she should take to be compliant with the policy. The method to ensure scope and focus is to be laser focused on the intent and ensure it is singularly related to the expected behavior. For example, rather than articulating the employees' responsibility and use of technology buried deep in a single policy as a section or paragraph, it is advised that a single acceptable use policy would be more appropriate. This way, the employee does not have to read a long policy to find what their responsibilities are, a single focused policy is more easily referenced, and, for management, enforced.

The general audience of the policy is the employee population, but there may be particular or specific group that the policy is intended for. The audience may be subcategorized as management, technical staff, and end users. Establishing an information security policy is very much an issue of corporate culture. Each one of these target audiences are affected by the policy in different ways. Managers not only are required to follow the policy themselves, but also are expected to enforce the policy as part of their managerial duties and responsibilities. Technical staff are expected to translate the policy into functional processes or automated controls, or a mix of both. The end user population is expected to follow the policies that are most relevant or directed toward their behavior with technology.

The degree of detail and length is typically dependent on the type of policy and target audience. Organizational policies should be written at a high enough level that are enduring and do not require frequent changes. Policies should be universal enough to accommodate organizational changes such as mergers, acquisitions, and divestitures with little need to update or modify the policies outside of scheduled reviews. Organizational policies should be only two to three pages in length—who is responsible for what—with a corporate officer or other appropriate senior manager signing off on the policy to give it the proper authority. Policies may also refer to the subordinate standards, procedures, or guidelines associated with the high-level policy. Standards, as more detailed forms of policy, are often operational or technical requirements, such as controls or control objectives. Policies that combine high-level statements of intent with detailed standards result in a complex document that may create problems with employee receptiveness and understanding, as well as issues when third parties, such as customers, that require the company to disclose policies. These requests result in the company having to produce more information than it is comfortable with disclosing. It is a best practice to limit the detail in high-level policies and let the subordinate policy types, such as standards or procedures, carry the additional detail on how the policy is being implemented.

Company information systems security policies need to be easily understood and practical to be effective. When writing the policy, it is equally important to set the correct tone for making the policy palatable and increase the chances of receptiveness. A draconian, harsh policy may alienate the employee population and increase the potential for nonadherence. An inappropriately weak-worded policy will simply cause benign neglect. Employee acceptance is dependent on the policy's ability to link the benefit of following policy to information systems security. A clear, concise, coherent, and consistent policy that sets expectations is more likely to be followed. This is where the technical writer and business representative reviews become critical in the development of the policy. They ensure that the information security policy does not become excessively technical or steeped in the jargon of information security. A good policy should be understandable to the general employee population.

Information systems security policies should provide the conditions for exceptions, when appropriate. An acceptable policy contains policy statements, but also should refer to the process of how exceptions can be granted. This ensures that the company policy is clearly stated and enforced, while providing a mechanism for dealing with exceptions without weakening the policy. Employees who are faced with a compliance challenge will have a choice to ignore the policy altogether. Without an exception clause in the policy, the employee may simply default to ignoring it.

Lastly, a compliance "grace period" is recommended by the policy development team. Companies do not issue policies and become compliant overnight. A grace period provides an acceptable period of time until when compliance can be measured. The IT department and business policies can review them, communicate the policy, implement them where applicable, and validate them for effectiveness prior to formal inspection. It is also a good practice to coordinate the grace period with Internal Audit during policy development how soon they anticipate auditing the policy after publication. Depending on the scope, scale, and impact of the policy, and the size of the company, a grace period may typically span several months up to 1 year.

Policy Publication

Once the policy is ready for review, it will follow the established governance process and be distributed to the companion IT departments for their review and concurrence. Once the IT department is satisfied with the policy in a finalized version, it is submitted to the centralized policy management group. The policy manager group then staffs the policy with the relevant corporate functions and business leadership representatives. The corporate functions (e.g., HR, Legal, Audit) may simply ask who was involved in the drafting of the policy and then confer with the appropriate development team member if there are any issues or criticisms. As the representative was part of the original authors, this is a relatively short conversation. However, some corporate functions may assign an independent reviewer who was not on the original development team to test for conformance. Similar to the corporate function review, the business leadership may quickly approve the policy if the development team included business partner participation. If not, then the business leadership review will entail a more detailed review to gain their approval. The business leadership has an equally valid reason for conducting such a detailed review—a policy that is either generally not acceptable to the business or lacks business support is a policy that will not be easily adopted or enforced. Once the policy management team has completed the socialization and staffing of the proposed policy, the document can be deemed ready for formal release.

Once formally accepted and promulgated, as documents, polices should be electronically published so that they are easily accessible to all employees. Large companies will have an organized policy repository on their company intranet available for download, printing, and saving. Typically, the information security function's intranet site will also link to these repositories. For those smaller organizations or companies, the information security function may host their policies on their own internal site.

The next step in publication is to communicate the policy. An effective policy communication strategy will ensure that all targeted audiences are aware of new or updated security policies, know where to find them, and understand how to comply with them and the consequences of nonadherence. However, the decision becomes should the policy be communicated to the entire employee population or a subset of those employees most affected by the policy. Large companies struggle with how to communicate policies, but for information security policies, the communication approach should be a tailored communication strategy approach such that the targeted employee population or group would receive directly only those policies needed. For example, corporate functions receive policy communication relative to the business process they govern or oversee. Technical staff would receive communication on those policies, standards, and procedures relevant to their area of technology management. The employees receive communications about their responsibilities to protect information assets.

TIP

An effective manner of communicating information security policy is through the establishment of annual security education and awareness training. Most organizations use the common learning platform to host mandatory annual training on information security where policies are communicated to all employees. The additional benefit of annual security education and awareness training is that many compliance requirements, such as PCI or HIPAA, also require annual training. Annual training can be the most effective and economical manner of communicating all information security policy requirements.

Policy Management

All information security policies should be reviewed and updated regularly. An annual review ensures the policy stays current, relevant, and up to date. Ad hoc updates may be necessary when a significant fundamental change in technology, process, or organizational realignment affects the relevancy or applicability of the existing policy, or parts of them. The review process should follow the initial development process as a matter of process integrity. However, the review may be significantly shorter if the policy does not require major updates or changes.

There are two important aspects that should be considered in the policy review. First, input from those most affected by the policy should be surveyed on the acceptance and efficacy of the policy. Business representatives, either as members of the original policy development team or independent of that effort, should be asked if the policy has made the desired effect based on intent. Technical staff should be interviewed on the experience of working with the existing policy; this can identify the technical difficulty, cost, or complexity of actual implementation and maintenance. Feedback will be useful to identify any necessary tailoring or adjustments that would make the policy more effective relative to the intent.

A second aspect is the identification of frequent audit nonconformance or security violations or that occurred over the life of the policy. Audit nonconformance information will identify where the policy was difficult to implement or enforce. Frequent policy violations that resulted in security events should be particularly noted. This information is an important indicator that the policy has some issues with its effectiveness. It may be that the policy is not feasible or capable to meet the original intent or may indicate that there are some simple adjustments that need to be made to refine the policy's implementation. While tuning the policy to make it more effective, the information security team should guard from watering down the policy's intent. Changing an effective policy to an ineffective policy, just to suit a particular need to reduce violations, only creates bad policy.

Once the review process is completed, the results should be documented in the policy itself, usually a revision and change section of the policy document. The aggregate decisions to update, retire, or keep the same policy in place should also be documented in some form, usually in the review team's meeting minutes. Then the same steps followed in the initial policy publication and communication should be followed for consistency. However, it may be much more simplified as a simple email to the targeted audiences; if there were no changes, the policy management team may decide a formal notification is unnecessary.

Policy Retirement

With the speed and changing landscape of technology, policies eventually become outdated or irrelevant. During a policy review, it is possible that the review team and stakeholders have arrived at a decision for whatever reason that the policy is no longer relevant and should be retired. However, once the policy has been identified as needing to be retired, the process is not to simply delete the policy document from the policy repository. A retirement process should involve a record of decision to retire, usually in the policy review team's meeting minutes. The policy itself should have a record of its retirement in the revision and change section of the policy document. The communication of the policy retirement should be made to the proper target audiences, and lastly, wherever polices are stored and listed, it may be appropriate to annotate "retired" next to the policy title.

SUMMARY

A well-designed information security policy framework outlines and defines the objectives of the organization's information protection strategy and delivers a stated approach to achieve these objectives. An information system without security policies is more likely to be a disjoint collection of statements, controls, and procedures that may not meet the information security protection objectives. Business aligned and relevant information security policies, then, can often be used to help integrate the multiple aspects of an enterprise information security program to achieve business objectives.

ACTIONS

Assess and align information security to the organization's culture.

- Identify the key elements of the organizational business model, structure, and culture. Aligning security as a "value add" in maintaining compliance to external and internal policies, regulations and statues, as well managing information security risks to business disruption.

Gain management commitment to information security policy intent.

■ Management commitment to security is essential to promote the importance of the information security policy, if not the most important factor in its adoption. Without management support, their employees are less likely to follow the policy. Management support of
information security policies provides the visibility and importance with their subordinate
manager and employees. The best time to obtain visibility for information security policy
conformance is at the initial publication and when a violation occurs. Management emphasis on the importance of conforming to policy and the consequences of a violation has the
effect of applying pressure to motivate all employees toward compliance. Management can
drive adoption by championing the resulting policies and putting their weight behind them
through leading by example.

Ensure that the information security policies are relevant.

■ Policies must be realistic, relevant, and appropriate. Once employees understand that the
information security policy helps them in their daily work activities to protect themselves
and the company information assets, they are much more likely to be receptive to be compliant. Likewise, when management realizes that the information security policy is leverage
to ensure adherence to legal or contractual requirements, managers are much more likely
to be supportive in providing resources for policy development and more inclined to become
policy champions themselves.

Maintain the currency of the information security policies.

■ All companies need to periodically review their information security policies. Failure to conduct periodic reviews will cause the policies to become outdated and lapse into obsolesce.
Similar to relevancy, employees will simply ignore or disregard policy requirements and, as
unrealistic and obsolete, become unenforceable. Beyond periodic reviews, an alternative is
to specify a defined review cycle more frequent than the annual review. By specifying a more
frequent review cycle, the policy has less opportunity to become stale.

Deliver information security policies that carry weight.

■ Information security teams worry that the policies that took an incredible amount of time to
formulate, socialize, and publish are not taken seriously. This is a common fear for
those information security teams that are new to the policy development practice or
where a policy management process is absent. This is where effective communication and
management commitment come into play. Effective communication ensures that employees understand the intent and importance of the policy to protect information assets.
Management commitment, as described earlier, enforces the importance of the security
policy to the employees, as well as the consequences of nonconformance. If both are present, employees will understand that these policies are not trivial and carry enough weight to
adopt the proper behaviors.

CHAPTER 5

Manage the Risks

INFORMATION IN THIS CHAPTER:

- Develop a risk management framework
- Evaluate objectives for risk management
- Responding to the results of risk assessments
- Communicating risk to the business
- Risk management and controls
- Gaining management buy in
- Actions

DEVELOP A RISK MANAGEMENT FRAMEWORK

One of the first objectives in risk management is to decide on what we will use for a framework or, perhaps, to develop one of our own. We need a framework to develop discipline and structure and to ensure integration with the system development life cycle (SDLC). There are a great many frameworks that we can make use of, with some of the most used being those from the National Institute for Science and Technology (NIST) and the International Organization for Standardization (ISO).

NOTE

The sharp-eyed reader may have noticed that the International Organization for Standardization does not fit well with ISO. ISO, in fact, is not an acronym at all, but is named for the Greek word "*isos*," which means equal. If ISO was an acronym, it would need to be changed for each language in which it was used, as the words would not always be used in the same order. This would not be very supportive of the mission for international standards.

Why We Need a Framework

Proceeding off on our risk management journey is a bit akin to heading off on a road trip into unfamiliar territory with no map or Global Positioning System.

Building a Practical Information Security Program. http://dx.doi.org/10.1016/B978-0-12-802042-5.00006-8

We might get there eventually, but it will not be an efficient or effective route for our journey.

Discipline and Structure

A framework provides us with discipline and structure for our program. It ensures that our risk management efforts are both consistent and repeatable. It ensures we will cover what we need as it has been through industry-wide peer review. If we cannot hand our framework to two different people and get generally the same results back from them, then we have more work to do on it.

A framework also aids us in documenting our efforts. If we do not follow a consistent path through risk management, then when we try to look back at historical data it will be very hard to assemble any sort of a coherent picture as we will be all over the map. This documentation is key when later we must deal with audits or compliance.

A key area we need to build our frameworks around is development of new capabilities or applications. As we look at how code is developed into capabilities it is important to remember that if security is not designed in at the beginning it will be both more expensive and less effective to add at the end.

SDLC Integration

Our risk management program and information security program should integrate closely with the SDLC. This integration will help to ensure that, as systems are built according to the SDLC, we have quantified and set a direction for handling any risks that are identified, which also plays very nicely into the information security program.

If we use the NIST definitions for both the risk management:

- Categorize
- Select
- Implement
- Assess
- Authorize
- Monitor

and the SDLC:

- Initiate
- Design
- Implement
- Operations and maintenance
- Dispose

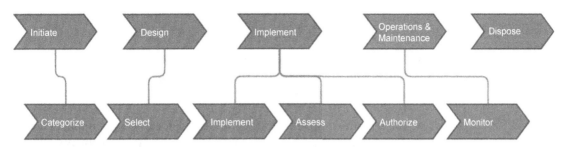

FIGURE 5.1
Risk and SDLC processes.

cycles, we can see, as in Fig. 5.1, how they can fit very nicely together.

When used in conjunction, these two processes pair up sets of activities well. When we are initiating our system, we are also categorizing it to enable later risk activities. When we are designing the system, we are also selecting the security controls that go into it. When we are implementing the system, we are also implementing the required controls, assessing their implementation and use, and authorizing the system. In the operations and maintenance phase, we monitor the controls in place on an ongoing basis.

An additional step, not covered in the risk management phases for NIST but covered in the SDLC steps, is disposal. We should, from a risk management perspective, be matching up disposal of obsolete controls with the disposal phase of the SDLC.

Choosing an Existing Framework
Given the wide variety of risk management frameworks available, in most cases it will be advisable to use one of the existing selections. Among the commonly used are NIST, ISO, and, in the case of certain federal systems, Federal Information Processing Standard (FIPS). Many organizations will end up using one or more of these as a basis, where appropriate. Several of these overlap in a complementary fashion and are by no means exclusive of each other. Although the ISO standards tend more in the direction of a checklist, NIST offers more of a practical set of implementation guides.

National Institute for Science and Technology
The NIST Special Publication provides guidance for a great many areas of computing and technology, including risk management. The two main publications in this area are SP 800-37 "Guide for Applying the Risk Management Framework to Federal Information Systems" and SP 800-53 "Security and Privacy Controls for Federal Information Systems and Organizations."

SP 800-37 lays out the risk management framework, the six steps that are the basis for many risk management programs:

- Categorize—Categorize the system based on the information that it handles and the impact of exposing or losing such data.
- Select—Select controls based on the categorization and any extenuating circumstances.
- Implement—Implement the controls and document the implementation.
- Assess—Assess the controls to ensure that they are implemented properly and performing as expected.
- Authorize—Authorize the use of the system based on the risk and the controls implemented to mitigate it.
- Monitor—Monitor the controls to ensure that they continue to appropriately mitigate risk.

SP 800-53 serves to provide control information for those who are selecting controls using SP 800-37 as a basis.

International Organization for Standardization

The ISO is a body first created in 1926 to set standards between nations. Among the over 21,000 standards that they have created are standards "covering almost every industry, from technology, to food safety, to agriculture and healthcare" [1].

In the case of risk management, ISO 31000:2009 "Risk Management - Principles and Guidelines" is the ISO standard governing this area. This standard "provides principles, framework and a process for managing risk" [2]. Although the NIST and FIPS documents are very much aimed at federal information systems, the ISO standard is intended for as broad as possible an audience.

Additionally, ISO Guide 73:2009 "Risk management – Vocabulary" works well with ISO 31000 by providing a standardized vocabulary for such efforts, and 31010:2009 "Risk management – Risk Assessment Techniques" focuses on the risk assessment process.

Federal Information Processing Standard

NIST maintains a series of publications, the FIPS documents. One of the directives of NIST, mandated by the Federal Information Security Management Act (FISMA) is to develop implementation guidance for federal information systems. At a federal system level, some of the NIST publications have the power of federal mandates.

The FIPS publications cover a wide area, but two in particular, FIPS 199 and FIPS 200, both mandatory standards, which are related to risk management frameworks.

FIPS 199 "Standards for Security Categorization of Federal Information and Information Systems" defines the categories of information systems to be used by the federal government. The categorization requirements under FIPS 199 include rating each system according to the confidentiality, integrity, and availability (CIA) triad.

FIPS 200 "Minimum Security Requirements for Federal Information and Information Systems" defines the minimum standards for security of federal systems. Essentially, it requires FIPS 199 to be used to categorize the system, then controls to be implemented to secure it appropriately, using NIST Special Publication 800-53 "Security and Privacy Controls for Federal Information Systems and Organizations" as a basis.

Although many of the FIPS documents fall back onto NIST publications as the basis of their efforts, they are somewhat of an extension of those publications that expands on and solidifies those requirements for systems needing a higher level of security.

Developing a Framework From Scratch

We can certainly develop our own framework or modify an existing one, if this is something that we think that we need to do, but we should think carefully before we proceed to do so. As we just finished discussing, there are numerous frameworks for risk management that already exist in the market. These frameworks have all undergone considerable review and testing and have been in use for years. Although reinventing the wheel may be merited in some cases, this seems like an unlikely candidate for such.

Presuming that we do decide that this effort makes sense, it would make sense to harvest whatever we can from the existing frameworks in building our own. Although we may build or tune a framework out of our own needs, most of the concepts behind the steps are likely to turn out very similar.

EVALUATE OBJECTIVES FOR RISK MANAGEMENT

There are two main categories of objectives for risk management as pertains to information security: the objectives of the business itself and the objectives that are specific to information security. In the business sense, we have the traditional objectives: strategic, financial, operational, and compliance. In the information security world, we have objectives that have come down from the business and those that are specific to security itself. These objectives are generally set during annual planning processes and added to or updated throughout the year on an as-needed basis.

Business Objectives

Our business objectives, as pertaining to risk management, can be categorized as strategic, financial, operational, or compliance related. As we will discuss later in this chapter in greater detail, our responses to these types of risk are to avoid, mitigate, accept, or transfer risk. These responses may be coordinated by a central group, or responsibility for resolution may fall to certain areas or lines of business.

Strategic

Strategic risks are those that result from uncertainties, unpursued areas, and general gaps in organizational strategies. These types of risks are usually external to the company and, thus, are often not included in or evaluated along with the more obvious and largely internal set of risks as we are evaluating risk. Some examples of strategic risk might include:

- a new competitor entering the market;
- an existing competitor developing a disruptive technology;
- changes to customer base or demand for a product;
- mergers and acquisitions among competitors.

Objectives for strategic risk are designed to enhance the corporate strategy and ensure that we are able to execute on it and gain the maximum level of effectiveness from it. Preparing responses to strategic risk can often be difficult as the risks are considerably more ethereal in nature than the other types that we need to deal with and develop strategies to compensate for.

Financial

Financial risks are those that are associated with the financial systems of the company, including how we conduct our financial operations on a day-to-day basis. Some examples of financial risk might include:

- cash flow
- who we owe money to and who owes money to us
- financial insurance or lack thereof
- interest rates
- exchange rates in foreign markets
- dependencies on single markets or customers

Financial risks, unlike strategic risks, are often very well defined and controlled. In some cases depending on how our organization is structured and owned, we will be subject to a number of laws and regulations that very specifically govern how we handle financial risk and how we report this to investors, customers, and the general public.

Operational

Operational risk objectives are those that are associated with the day-to-day operation of the business and its operational and administrative processes and procedures. These are typically managed at a line of business level as they require considerable domain knowledge of the business to properly respond to the individual risk. Some examples of operational risk might include:

- hiring processes
- termination processes
- supply chain
- management of IT networks and systems
- management of theft or loss
- management of fraud

Operational objectives, and their associated risks, are, to a large extent, the underpinning of our strategic objectives. For example, if our IT systems cannot support the amount of traffic that results from the heightened level of activity during our annual black Friday [1] sale, then we may potentially lose tens of millions of dollars of sales and be unable to support our strategic objective for sales.

Compliance

Compliance risk objectives are those associated with our requirements to comply with the laws and regulations that are defined by the industries and geographies in which we are operating. In particular, when we are operating internationally, this can result in a very complex set of compliance boundaries in which we must conduct business. Ensuring proper compliance is one of the primary objectives of being a strong corporate governance program. Some examples of compliance risk might include:

- new laws around health or safety (tobacco, asbestos);
- changes in legislation reducing demand for a product;
- costs associated with compliance assessments and resulting mitigation efforts;
- higher operational costs resulting from regulatory changes;
- changing laws on what information needs to be reported and tracked.

Compliance risks can weigh heavily on our strategic and financial objectives as they have the ability to heavily influence both of these areas. A change to compliance can heavily impact business, for example, the announcement from the Payment Card Industry (PCI) council in 2011 [2] that required retailers to start supporting EMV (Europay, MasterCard, Visa)-enabled payment cards in 2015, causing retailers to upgrade payment terminals en masse.

Security Objectives

The management of information security risk and the resulting objectives are centered on protecting the organization and its information assets from harm, whether accidental or intentional. These objectives fall into two major categories: those inherited from the business, as just discussed, and those that are specific to information security.

Objectives Inherited From the Business

Information security objectives inherited from the business include support of strategic, financial, operational, and compliance areas. Although this does not mean that information security is directly responsible for executing these objectives, it does mean that we are responsible for supporting the organization in its safe execution of them. Ultimately, if we allow the organization's assets confidentiality, integrity, or availability to be compromised, it will adversely affect its ability to conduct business.

Strategic

As discussed earlier, strategic risks are those that result from uncertainties, unpursued areas, and general gaps in organizational strategies and they are largely external to the organization. In an information security sense, much of our responsibility here will likely be in the area of protecting the organization and its information assets from external interference. Particularly in the case where we have trade secrets or other intellectual property on which the company depends on maintaining a high level of confidentiality around, the information security team has a definite role here.

Financial

When we covered this risk earlier in the chapter, we said that financial risks are those that are associated with the financial systems of the company, including how we conduct our financial operations on a day-to-day basis. Security has a large role here, particularly in the area of keeping attackers from compromising the systems on which our company's finances run or interact with.

Operational

As discussed, operational risk objectives are those that are associated with the day-to-day operation of the business and its operational and administrative processes and procedures. Again, as with financial objectives, it falls within information security's remit to protect the operational systems of the company. If we do not protect our IT systems, supply chains, etc., then the ability of our organization to conduct business will be highly impacted. We also need to make sure that security does not obstruct operations, or security will simply not be consulted in the future.

Compliance

When we look at compliance, our risk objectives are those associated with our requirements to comply with the laws and regulations that are defined by the industries and geographies in which we are operating. This is an area heavily associated with information security, as many of the controls that we are required to put in place from a mitigation perspective are very specifically security controls. In many cases, it falls to the security department to assess what controls are needed, ensure that they are put in place, and evaluate their proper functionality after they are implemented.

Security-Specific Objectives

In a strong security program, our security-specific goals for risk management will be constructed based on the business, the structure of the organization, the risks identified, and the resources that we have available to work with. In many cases, the majority of the high-level objectives for information security will be driven by the requirements of the business. In a security-specific sense, we can structure our efforts around the CIA triad.

Confidentiality

Maintaining confidentiality is a key information security task in almost any industry or environment that we might care to examine. Even in the case where we are not working with any sort of regulated data, which is somewhat of a rare business environment these days, we will generally have some information that we would not care to have publicized, even if it is only lists of customers or clients that competitors might make use of. Many such efforts around confidentiality will be focused on the securing of data within our systems and movement of data into, out of, and among the systems that we control ourselves and those external systems that we interface with.

Integrity

Protecting the integrity of our information assets is another area in which information security plays a key role. If we lose control of the way in which our data are manipulated and enable unauthorized or unintentional manipulation of data, this may have a very large effect on the business.

A good example of this is the Wal-Mart Universal Product Code (UPC) label manipulation scam, an uncomfortably often repeated scam in which attackers overlay the UPC barcode on more expensive items with those from similar but less expensive items [5]. This is a particularly difficult area to secure, as the information defining which product is being purchased and what said product should cost is easily open to modification.

Availability

The availability of our applications, systems, networks, and other items of infrastructure can have great impact on our ability to conduct business and often falls, at least in part, under the purview of information security. Although, conceptually, this is not a difficult thing, it can be a considerably more complex area than we might expect it to be. When we have even a small number of internal and external systems interacting to build software, maintain system configurations, take payments from customers, ship products, and so on, making sure that these systems are always up and functioning and can fail over properly can be a large task and should not be underestimated.

RESPONDING TO THE RESULTS OF RISK ASSESSMENTS

As we look at responding to the results of our risk assessments, two major questions arise: who decided how we will respond to the risks that we have codified and in what ways can we respond to the risks? Although the answer to the first can be somewhat fluid, depending on our organization, the latter has a well-structured set of methods by which we can respond.

Who Decides How to Respond?

When we look to place responsibility for deciding how to respond to risk with a particular team or group within the organization, there are a number of places that this could land. We could make use of a risk management team, leave decision making to the lines of business that own the risks, information security could handle risk, or we could form a collaborative group expressly for doing so.

Centralized Risk Groups

In larger, more mature, and more well-structured organizations, we are very likely to find a group whose charter is to manage risk for the overall organization. Such a group will typically be part of legal, human resources, or even report through information security itself.

The benefit of having a risk team be responsible for deciding how to respond to risks is that tasks like this are, presumably, very specifically why such a team exists. They have the expertise and domain knowledge of risk management and can apply this, in conjunction with knowledge of the organization, to responding to the risks that have been identified.

Presuming an organization with the size and resources to support a risk organization, tasking them with developing the strategy for responding to risks would seem to be the most efficient and logical path.

Lines of Business

Another option that we have is to assign the responsibility for deciding how to respond to risks to the lines of business from which said risks issued, given that the lines of business have intimate knowledge of their procedures and processes and will have, perhaps, the best handle on what needs to be done to resolve this risk. This would make a certain amount of sense.

One potential issue here, especially in larger organizations, is that we may be dealing with many lines of business, perhaps distributed over large geographic areas. Even in the case where we let the businesses manage their own risks, we would still need some sort of central body to manage the decentralized set of groups that would be handling all of the different risks.

Absent of this function, we would not have a good way of being able to track the response to the risks and ensure that they were taken care of appropriately.

Information Security

We might also decide to leave the decisions regarding how to respond to risk to the information security team. After all, the security team will have a good handle on the security intricacies surrounding the risks and should play a large part in deciding how to handle the identified risks.

A potential issue with this approach is that information security is often located in one of a couple portions of the organization, either reporting directly to the C-level executives, or reporting up through the information technology leadership. Although supporting information security with its very focused and often very technology-oriented mission works well from these two reporting paths, it can sometimes give security a bit of a myopic view of the overall organization.

Collaborative Groups

We might also elect to form a collaborative group to decide how to respond to risk. An interdisciplinary team composed of risk management, the lines of business, information security, and perhaps other representatives from information technology or elsewhere in the company can come together to form a very knowledgeable team that is capable of putting together a very solid plan for handling risks.

Although the other teams that we have looked at all have their strengths, any of them attempting to work in isolation may not ultimately fare well. Each of them, by themselves, will end up missing some level of the knowledge and expertise needed to properly respond to risks as they are discovered. Additionally, this type of structure will usually work well with any size and structure of organization. The difference being the scale of the team and the degree to which its members are specialized. In smaller organizations, we are likely to see such teams composed of fewer people with a broader range of responsibilities.

Ultimately who accepts risk is also based on the amount of risk. A security engineer or incident response analyst could decide how to deal with risk of isolated infected system but only the chief executive officer would decide how to respond to a breach of all customer data. Defining roles is key to make sure the right level of the organization is making appropriate decisions.

Types of Responses

There are four ways that we can respond to risk. We can avoid it, we can mitigate it, we can accept it, or we can transfer it to someone else. Which type of

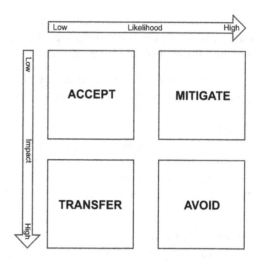

FIGURE 5.2
Responses to risk.

response to use should be based on an assessment of the likelihood of the risk occurring and the impact the risk will have if it does actually occur, as shown in Fig. 5.2.

Avoid
If the risk has a high likelihood of occurring and a high impact if it does occur, we should avoid the risk in question entirely. Although this gives us a very sure method of not needing to deal with the risk, it can be a very expensive proposition indeed.

For example, retail establishments that take credit card payments can assume a truly staggering level of risk by doing so. With thousands or millions of customer credit card numbers traversing hosts and networks on their way to be processed, we provide a target rich environment for attackers looking to steal such data for fraudulent purposes. We can avoid this risk by using tokens to represent the credit card numbers instead of using the numbers themselves. If we no longer handle credit card numbers directly, we no longer have a risk.

NOTE

A token is the "process by which the primary account number (PAN) is replaced with a surrogate value called a *token*. Detokenization is the reverse process of redeeming a token for its associated PAN value. The security of an individual token relies predominantly on the infeasibility of determining the original PAN knowing only the surrogate value." [3].

Mitigate

In cases where our risk has a high likelihood of occurring, but a low impact, the best route of response is to put controls in place to mitigate the risk. Although we can mitigate a risk, we can almost never eliminate it entirely. Whatever risk we have left after putting controls in place to mitigate it is known as residual risk.

We should also carefully evaluate the cost of mitigating the risk versus the cost of just accepting it. We can certainly put a very strong set of controls in place to secure a particular set of data by encrypting the individual items of data in a database, encrypting the storage on the database servers, putting numerous firewalls and intrusion detection systems on the carefully segmented network to which the computer is connected and locking the whole lot away inside a high-security facility with armed guards. However, if the data in question is mom's chocolate chip cookie recipe, there was no real cost in just accepting the risk in the first place. It can be easy to lose sight of this.

Accept

If a risk has a low likelihood of occurring and a low level of impact if it does occur, then we may simply choose to accept the risk.

For example, the majority of states in the United States require vehicle owners to purchase car insurance, which can be costly depending on the type of vehicle in question and the driving record of the vehicle owner. The cases in which it might be noticed that there is no insurance covering a vehicle would be if the vehicle was in an accident or if the vehicle was pulled over by the police and they request proof of insurance. For most careful drivers, the chance of either of these situations taking place is relatively low. Although illegal, we might choose not to purchase insurance on the basis of the likelihood of getting caught being relatively low and the impact of getting caught (outside of the cost of an accident) still costing less than buying proper insurance.

Acceptance of a risk because it is unlikely to occur does come with one caveat; we need to carefully monitor the risk for signs that its likelihood or impact have changed. Accepting a risk and then ignoring it for an extended period of time is almost sure to have undesirable results.

Transfer

In the case of risks that have a low probability of occurring, but can have a high impact, the best response may be to transfer the risk. Transferring the risk may mean asking another party to conduct the risk activity in our place, or could also include purchasing insurance to offset the cost of dealing with the risk, should it actually arise.

Transferring risk to another organization, in terms of depending on them to run part of your technology infrastructure is, in theory, supposed to be a positive thing for an organization. Unfortunately, this is not always the case. In mid-2015, eCellar Systems, a company that processes payments for a number of wineries in Northern California, announced a breach in which "The intruder gained access to customer names, credit/debit card numbers, the related billing addresses, and any dates of birth in our system during the window of April 1st through 30th this year," [4]. Among other issues, it turned out that eCellar did not use a tokenization solution to protect the credit cards in its systems, thus rendering an attack directed at stealing this sort of information very fruitful.

Cyber liability insurance is another form of risk transference. An organization can purchase "insurance designed to cover consumers of technology services or products. More specifically, the policies are intended to cover a variety of both liability and property losses that may result when a business engages in various electronic activities, such as selling on the Internet or collecting data within its internal electronic network" [5], thus insulating themselves from the impact of incidents that might occur.

COMMUNICATING RISK TO THE BUSINESS

When we communicate risk to the business, it will pay dividends to plan out how exactly we will do so in advance. We need to know what our channels of communication will be, how we will alert them to issues or changes, how we will communicate responsibilities to users, and how we will receive communication from users.

Communications Channels

When we are planning to communicate to the business and/or its members, we need to understand how exactly this mechanism will work. It is helpful to know who exactly the stakeholders are for the area in which we will be communicating, to have an understanding of how the businesses are structured and what they do, and we need to be able to tailor our communications for those audiences so that they are properly understood and relevant.

Understand the Business

Understanding the business is the first and, perhaps, the most crucial part of the information that we need to successfully communicate with them. Without an idea of how the organization is structured in terms of what the hierarchy is and which pieces do what, we will have very little on which to base critical communications, as we will not know what needs to be communicated to which parts of the organization.

Once we have some idea of the organizational structure and know which pieces of the company do what, we can start to sort out who exactly it is that we need to communicate to get tasks and projects accomplished.

Know Who the Stakeholders Are

When looking to communicate with the lines of business, as mentioned, it is vital to know who it is that we are looking to communicate to. Knowing who the stakeholders are is a critical part of this. We need to know, for each portion of the organization, who the leadership is and who it is within each leadership chain that we need to be communicating with on a given issue. Once we know who the stakeholders are, we can tune our communication to them to be more effective.

Targeting Communication

In addition to knowing who it is that we should be talking to, it is also import-ant to understand at what level we should approach the subparts of the organi-zation for a given issue. If we are taking detailed technical issues to the senior management for a segment of the business, then we are probably approaching the wrong level. These managers will end up directing us to someone below them, possibly several levels down, until we arrive at the proper person to help us. Likewise, approaching the bottom level of management for high-level stra-tegic decisions is equally likely to fail.

Alerting for Issues or Changes

In communicating with users, we need to plan for what processes and mecha-nisms we will use to communicate alerts. Is it likely that, at some point, we will have to communicate the need for a change to be made in the environment, or alert users to an issue, for example, patching on workstations or servers of a critical vulnerability.

Alerting Mechanisms

When we choose alerting mechanisms, we have a few options, many of which fall into the realm of normal communication in the organization, such as email. The unfortunate case, especially in larger organizations, is that using a common method of communication for alerting may mean that our alerts will get lost in the massive tsunami of meeting requests, email exhorting us to con-tribute to the charity of the day, and the multitude of other corporate chatter. If we expect anyone to actually take action, we will need to do something that makes our messages stand out from the rest.

Conspicuous Alerting

For our alerts to be seen and acted upon, we need to make them stand out from the crowd. We can do this in a few ways:

- Uncommon senders—If we send email from a standard corporate distribution list it is unlikely to be noticed. Email from the vice president over information technology may fare better.
- Crafted subjects—Messages sent with strong subjects suggesting action, such as "action required" may gain us a bit more notice.

■ Out of band—Any other mechanisms we can use to communicate our messages may increase its effectiveness, for example, having managers directly pass the information to their employees in person.

Alert Fatigue

When we are subjected to a constant barrage of alerts particularly those that are, or at least seem to be, of a less than worthwhile nature, we develop what is known as "alert fatigue" or "alarm fatigue" [7]. Alert fatigue desensitizes us to the alerting mechanism in general, greatly increasing the likelihood that we will ignore the alarm entirely.

In the case of the Target breach that occurred in 2014, Target's information security team was alerted, repeatedly, to the malware that was part of the attack, but chose to ignore it because the security tool alerting them was alerting on a very regular basis [8].

Communicating Responsibilities to Users

When we communicate with users, we need to be clear about what exactly it is that they are responsible for. For example, if we are sending out a "patch now" alert email and exhorting users to apply a critical Microsoft patch, we need to be clear on exactly what it is that we expect of them and who specifically is responsible for doing what.

Training and Awareness

Training and awareness, as we will discuss to a much greater extent in Chapter 8, plays a part in how we communicate to users. It gives us a chance to set a baseline for what we expect them to do, it lets us specify how it is that we will communicate with them, and it gives us the opportunity to send a message tuned for each audience on what their overall responsibilities are, as relates to information security. Leaders, IT staff, and users all need to have training tailored to their functions.

Accountability

As mentioned earlier, we need to be clear what exactly it is that those being communicated to are going to be held accountable for and what it is that we expect them to do. In our "patch now" email example earlier, we might specifically call out what actions we expected from end users, server administrators for different platforms, desktop support personnel, etc.

If we do not craft our message with this level of clarity, we will have a few people who do what we expect, a few people who take some unexpected action entirely, and the rest who will do nothing at all because they did not find a clear message that called for action from them directly. Where appropriate there should be consequences for not meeting expectations built into the Human Resources system.

Receiving Communications From Users

Equally as important to planning out how we will send communication to users and the businesses that they represent is how we will receive communication from users. We should understand what the communication mechanisms are from the user end to us and set expectations for how those communications will be responded to. We also need to have a plan for critical communications coming from the user end, such as those reporting security incidents. Automation is important to ensure timely response.

Communication Mechanisms

Mechanisms for communication from the user world may be slightly different than those that we are sending out. When we are on the sending end, the communication mechanism is many to one; we are typically sending out to a large group of people. On communications where we are on the receiving end, we have the opposite situation; many to one. Where we might be okay in sending out from a mailing list, being on the receiving end of one with a large user base on the other side may be problematic.

In this case, we will likely be better off in putting some sort of gating mechanism in place such as a ticketing system or help desk. In this way we can control and filter the incoming messages, perhaps solving the source of some of them simply by having a process in place to corral them on the way in.

Setting Expectations

Setting expectations for how we will respond to incoming communications is another important part of the process. These expectations may range anywhere from "we will respond to this request within X hours/days" to "this mailbox is unmonitored, please call the help desk for issues." The exact content of such replies does not matter as much as the fact that we have set the expectations for the person on the other end of the communication.

Another method of setting expectations is through the use of service level agreements (SLAs). When we document SLAs, we preset an expectation of how long we will take for a first response to a request, how often we will provide updates, and, potentially, the period of time in which we expect to solve the issue.

Incident Reporting

Security incident reporting is somewhat of a special case for user communication. This is an area in which we want to be sure to pay maximum attention to what users are communicating to us. Although there will be a certain number of false positives from end users, we would generally have them overreport than keep quiet about some sort of problem that was happening.

Issues in this area can generally be fixed with the application of a bit of process and training for both users and those performing intake of incidents. We need to quickly be able to triage the situation and decide whether the issue merits further action or simply needs to be routed elsewhere for a solution. This area needs training and validation exercises to ensure it is operating correctly.

RISK MANAGEMENT AND CONTROLS

In the world of risk management, controls provide us with one of our primary methods for mitigating risk. They help to assure us that our risk management requirements are being met from a legal, regulatory, and business standpoint. They ensure that the risks are being dealt with and that the controls that we put in place are adequate.

What Security Controls Provide Us

Ultimately, controls provide us with some assurance that our risks are being handled in some fashion. We need to make sure that we are in compliance with the various items under which we fall by dint of the data that we are handling and the industries in which we operate. They also help to give us some assurance that risks are being dealt with. This ties back to using frameworks that outline the proper controls.

Assurance That Requirements Are Met

Controls help to, but do not assure, that our requirements are being met. Often, our compliance requirements come along with specific requirements for controls being implemented. For instance, the PCI DSS (Payment Card Industry Data Security Standard) requirements include a variety of specific controls that need to be implemented, an example of which includes "5.1 Deploy antivirus software on all systems commonly affected by malicious software (particularly personal computers and servers)" [6].

Controls can fall into three main categories, physical, administrative, and technical. Physical controls mitigate risks to physical security, administrative controls mitigate risks from a procedural and process perspective, and technical controls manage risk from a technical standpoint. None of the categories of controls are sufficient by themselves, but each contributes to the layered defense necessary to provide good security.

Assurance That Risks Are Being Dealt With

Controls also provide us with some level of assurance that risks are being dealt with. In the sense of technical controls, this typically means that we are mitigating risk. We put firewalls, intrusion detection systems, access control lists, and so on in place to prevent attackers from getting into our systems at all.

In a certain sense, when we accept, avoid, or transfer risk, we may be utilizing administrative controls. We are putting processes, procedures, standards, etc. in place to prevent us from hurting ourselves by making bad decisions about taking risk.

We must also consider, however, that controls are only as good as our implementation of them. If we implement a control in an improper or insecure fashion then we may actually be worse off than not having implemented it at all, due to having given ourselves and our customers a false sense of security.

Key Controls

Key controls are the primary controls that we use to manage risk with our environments. Key controls typically have characteristics similar to the following:

- Key controls are required to provide some level of assurance that the risk will be mitigated.
- If the control fails, it is unlikely that another control could take over for it.
- If the control fails, it will affect an entire process.
- The control needs to be tested as part of compliance or audit efforts.

What is and is not a key control will vary by the environment in question and the risks within that particular environment. What is a key control in one place may not be so in another.

Establish

Establishing key controls will be a product of the risk management process, largely in our responses to risk. When we mitigate or transfer our risk, in particular, we will likely put controls in place around our efforts to ensure that we end up in an expected place.

As mentioned previously, key controls will vary from one environment to the next. Our particular set of key controls will be those that are needed to mitigate our risks, each control covering its own areas.

Evaluate

Key controls must be periodically evaluated to ensure that they are functioning in accordance with the requirements for putting them in place. In the case of technical controls, such as firewalls, this often involves penetration testing to have some level of assurance that the control is doing what it is supposed to do.

In the case of administrative controls, we will often need to run through the documentation that defines how the control should work and then provide examples of the process actually being followed in the intended fashion.

Effectiveness

The effectiveness of our controls is somewhat more difficult to gauge than the functionality of them as it is rather more subjective. In many cases, we should easily be able to accurately evaluate administrative controls as this involves working through the processes and comparing how they work on paper versus how they are implemented in practice.

Technical controls are somewhat a different case. Evaluating such tools will often require a highly technical and specialized set of skills and, sometimes, tooling and instrumentation as well. Outside of companies with a great deal of resources to spare on such activities, or those already operating in such industries, we will often need to outsource such evaluations.

Control Activities

When we have controls in place, there are three primary sets of activities that we need to do to maintain them properly: monitoring, reporting, and review. Each of these activities is equally important as the next and we will likely not have a full coverage of ensuring control health conducting all three.

Monitoring

Controls need to be monitored to determine whether the measures have the desired effect and whether they have a positive or a negative impact toward mitigating or reducing risk. Monitoring of controls, especially key controls, should be done on an ongoing basis to make sure that they stay current and continue to perform their role relative to changes in the environment or in technology. Without such monitoring, our controls will quickly fall out of usefulness and we may not even know that this has happened. Additionally, controls should be slated for recurring and regular review cycles.

Review

Our controls need to undergo a periodic review to determine whether they are still effective and meet the risk management objectives, control objectives, and the risk environment. In particular, as risks change, are negated, and new risks arise, these changes should be feeding directly into the review process. Without an ongoing feed of risk updates, and subsequent review to determine whether our set of controls still covers these risks, or whether new controls are needed entirely or old controls should be retired, we will again, fall quickly out of usefulness in the controls department.

Reporting

As we monitor controls and review them, we also need to document the results and carefully track how the control environment in our organization changes so that they can be tracked over longer periods of time and reported to management. Given a history of control change, we can begin to evaluate trends and, perhaps, begin to predict where the trends in our control changes are headed. This can be of great utility in forecasting resource needs as some controls are very expensive to make changes to.

Controls and Audit Findings

In many cases, audit findings are centered on the use of controls. For any given framework against which we might be audited, we are likely to find audit findings centered on controls or the lack of them, and how these controls are applied.

Auditing Against Frameworks

Audits are typically done against existing frameworks of some kind. In the security world, these will often take the form of the ISO 27000 series of documents or the NIST special publications series documents that cover various information security topics. There are a multitude of such frameworks against which we might be audited, and the particular one chosen by our auditors will vary with organization, industry, and other similar factors.

Audit Findings Centered on Controls

Audit findings are often centered on the use of controls. For any given framework against which we might be audited, said framework will generally specify a control or set of controls to mitigate particular risks. In an organization that deals with a variety of regulated data, we might even see the same or overlapping controls mandated by different bodies. This can be very complex to sort out when planning an information security program and, in the end, may not lead to a strong security program at all.

Auditing How Controls Are Applied

Another item of concern in many audits is how exactly our controls are applied or implemented. We could have the newest, most expensive, and strongest security controls available on the market, but if we have not implemented them properly, they may be of no use to us at all.

Auditors will typically have criteria for the appropriate implementation of particular controls, hopefully with a foundation in the particular framework being used to develop and assess the environment.

GAINING MANAGEMENT BUY IN

One of the most crucial aspects of an information security program, any part of it that we might care to examine, is gaining management buy in and support. If we are not adequately supported by management, then we will have difficulty in a wide variety of areas, whether gaining funding, staffing, resources, or even political support. Gaining such support will be considerably eased if we establish business relevancy, put issues into context, discuss our objectives and how to meet them, relate these objectives back to compliance, and communicate our needs, all backed with solid data. This may seem like a large effort, but really it is relatively simple, as shown in Fig. 5.3.

Establish Business Relevancy

A vital part of getting management buy in is establishing how our request is relevant to the business. A common mistake made by security professionals is to assume that information security exists for its own sake. Although it is true that security is important, outside of a few exceptions, it is not the primary driver for business. The primary business driver is selling the company's products like selling books, providing a mobile financial application for customer use, cleaning windows, etc. We need to address how it is that whatever we are asking for is going to drive business to the company or how it is going to prevent current business from leaving.

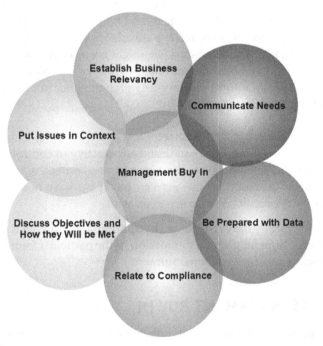

FIGURE 5.3

Gaining management buy in.

In many cases, drawing lines from information security to business objectives is relatively simple. Information security exists to protect customer data, safeguard intellectual property, protect infrastructure from attackers, and so on. Particularly in the case where we are in or adjacent to an industry where sensitive or regulated data are being handled, we have an easy answer to the "why do we need to do this?" question.

Discuss Objectives and How They Will Be Met

When we are presenting our plan to gain management buy in, it is vital that we discuss how it is that we plan to meet our objectives. This will often take the form of a project plan or set of documents that detail out what exactly it is that we are doing, what the timeline is for accomplishing our goals, what resources are to be used, what dependencies are in place both within and outside of our organization, and so on.

We should also be careful, as with any other of our set of details that describe our project, not to bring information to management at too great a level of depth. Not only do we need to have the detailed information that describes how we will execute our plan at the level that we need to accomplish it, but we also need to have a boiled up version, suitable for presenting to management, sometimes referred to as an executive summary. We will return to this concept again later in this section.

Relate to Compliance

One particularly helpful tactic to gain management buy in for our efforts is to relate them back to compliance. This does make the assumption that we are working with data that are, in some fashion regulated, but this is very common and not doing so in some portion of our environment would be the exception rather than the rule. Where there is no regulation there are still key stakeholder requirements and the list below can help determine what that looks like.

The wide variety of compliance-driven security efforts present in almost any given organization might include:

- PII—Personally Identifiable Information (name, address, Social Security number)
- PCI—Payment Card Industry (credit cards)
- HIPAA—Health Insurance Portability and Accountability Act (health care data)
- FERPA—Family Educational Rights and Privacy Act (educational data)
- GLBA—Gramm–Leach–Bliley Act (financial data)

Nearly any company with employees will have at least a few areas where one or other types of these data are stored. If we can relate our security efforts back to items that we are legally or contractually required to put protections in place for, this can considerably ease our task.

It is important to note that a security program based on the baseline compliance requirements is not necessarily a very secure program. Although these often represent a good starting point, they are not sufficient to provide strong security.

Be Prepared With Data

Although our need to display data at varying depths will change with the audience that we are presenting to, we should always be prepared to discuss it. In many cases, especially in larger organizations, the higher the level of management that we are presenting to, the less time and interest they will have in doing deep dives into our data. As with presentations of any kind, we need to have tuned our message to the audience, but be ready go deeper if needed.

As discussed in the earlier sections, among other things, we need to be able to establish business relevancy, put issues into context, and relate back to compliance. These are all data-driven items and we should have the information ready about what exactly needs to be done, what the results will be if we do not do it, and what is needed to achieve it.

When preparing data on which decisions will be made, it can often be helpful to present alternatives as well. In this way we can provide a minimum, adequate, and ideal set of plans, along with the data to back each of them up. One of the caveats with presenting data-backed requests is that data are very black and white and can lead to a yes or no answer that does not allow for grey areas, unless we present them.

Communicate Needs

When we are making a request of management, we need to be very careful to communicate our needs. As covered in the previous section, we need to have enough data to back up what it is that we are asking for, but we need to go beyond this when actually asking.

If our expectation is that we will need to spend 1 million dollars on a new cluster of security appliances, hire two people to run it, and send both of them to training classes from the vendor, then we need to ask for this in very specific terms. We need to have a write-up that covers why this was the selected solution, how it relates back to the objectives of the overall organization and its compliance efforts, and how exactly we plan to make the purchase, get it installed, and have it up and performing its function, all in conjunction with a set of milestones and a timeline for getting everything done.

ACTIONS

Establish a risk management framework

- Choose an existing framework or develop a custom framework

Evaluate objectives for risk management

- Evaluate business objectives
  - Strategic objectives
  - Financial objectives
  - Operational objectives
  - Compliance objectives
- Evaluate security objectives
  - Objectives inherited from the business
  - Security-specific objectives
- Plan risk communication to the business
  - Develop and document communication channels
  - Develop change and alerting mechanisms
  - Develop mechanism for receiving communication from users
  - Communicate responsibilities to users

Recommend appropriate controls to respond to risks

- Assist in developing key controls
- Conduct control activities
  - Monitoring
  - Reporting
  - Review

Get management buy in and direction

- Establish business relevancy
- Discuss objectives and how they will be met
- Relate activities back to compliance
- Be prepared with data
- Communicate needs

References

[1] Black Friday: definition of Black Friday in Oxford dictionary (American English) (US) [Internet]. Oxford University Press. Available: http://www.oxforddictionaries.com/us/definition/american_english/black-friday.

[2] Bartenstein C. EMV's Uncertain Fate in the US. In: Protean Payment [Internet]. Available: http://proteanpayment.org/?p=248.

[3] [Notitle][Internet].Available:https://www.pcisecuritystandards.org/documents/Tokenization_Guidelines_Info_Supplement.pdf.

[4] Breach at Winery Card Processor Missing Link — Krebs on Security [Internet]. Available: http://krebsonsecurity.com/2015/06/breach-at-winery-card-processor-missing-link/.

[5] Cyber and privacy insurance – Insurance Glossary | IRMI.com [Internet]. Available: https://www.irmi.com/online/insurance-glossary/terms/c/cyber-and-privacy-insurance.aspx.

[6] Official PCI Security Standards Council Site – Verify PCI Compliance, Download Data Security and Credit Card Security Standards [Internet]. Available: https://www.pcisecuritystandards.org/documents/PCI_DSS_v3-2.pdf.

[7] Alert Fatigue | AHRQ Patient Safety Network [Internet]. [cited 14 Sep 2016]. Available: https://www.psnet.ahrq.gov/primers/primer/28/alert-fatigue.

[8] Target Ignored Data Breach Alarms. In: Dark Reading [Internet]. [cited 14 Sep 2016]. Available: http://www.darkreading.com/attacks-and-breaches/target-ignored-data-breach-alarms/d/d-id/1127712.

CHAPTER 6

Protect the Data

INFORMATION IN THIS CHAPTER:

- Data classification
- Access control programs
- Physical and environmental security for facilities
- Zones of trust and control
- Ensuring data confidentiality
- Making use of existing technologies
- Actions

Protecting the information assets on which our organization runs is a large part of our responsibility as security professionals. For almost any organization we choose to look at, information is key to survival and growth. Even in the case where we look at a business much more oriented to the physical, manufacturing, for instance, where goods being created and then sold are the linchpin of the business, the information is still what drives the business. Our manufacturing business without its customer lists and the ability to bill its customers would not last for more than a quarter.

To protect these information assets, we need to understand what they are and what physical components they have, and be able to classify and be able to apply controls to both sides. In addition, we need to be concerned with technology areas changing and growing with rapidity such as the cloud, laptops, and mobile devices.

DATA CLASSIFICATION

Data classification gives us a way to indicate how a particular item of data should be stored, handled, and protected, who it should be shared with, and what the rules around sharing might be.

103

Building a Practical Information Security Program. http://dx.doi.org/10.1016/B978-0-12-802042-5.00007-X

When we look at types of data to classify them, they may fall into different categories of classification systems, depending on whether the environment in question is commercial or not.

Data Sensitivity and Criticality

The particular language used in classification systems for government and military use will vary from one country to another, but the concepts are, for the most part, the same. The system used in the United States contains the following commonly used classification levels (there are quite a few more):

- Top secret
  - the unauthorized disclosure of which reasonably could be expected to cause exceptionally grave damage to the national security
- Secret
  - the unauthorized disclosure of which reasonably could be expected to cause serious damage to the national security
- Confidential
  - the unauthorized disclosure of which reasonably could be expected to cause damage to the national security
- Unclassified
  - data open to the general public with no restrictions

Such systems are implemented in a strict method, with stiff penalties for not doing so or for not having done so.

In a corporate environment, we may find data marked with a classification system similar to what is used by the military, but with somewhat differing terminology:

- Highly sensitive/Restricted
  - could represent a very high cost if exposed or controlled by regulations
- Sensitive/Confidential
  - could represent a high cost if exposed
- Internal
  - data not for public consumption, but not of a sensitive nature
- Public
  - data for public consumption, as might be posted on a public website.

In a corporate environment, we will often find data classification schemes such as this, perhaps with some variation in exact terminology, implemented in policy but not in practice, or implemented in a poor manner. These environments are not often under any regulatory pressure to do so, and the task is a difficult one to carry out. The exception to this is in businesses dealing with or having had such work contracted to them.

In the case of regulatory data, we will often find data classified into the following categories:

- Personally Identifiable Information (PII)—name, address, social security number, etc.
- Patient Healthcare Information—health care data
- Payment Card Industry (PCI)—payment card data
- Family Educational Rights and Privacy Act—educational data

These classifications are not mutually exclusive with those above or with each other, and we may well find a combination of them, as we might in the case of a database containing customer data being marked as Highly Sensitive, PII, and PCI. Due to the regulatory nature of these categories, we will find them used to a much greater extent in corporate or educational settings than those in the aforementioned list.

ACCESS CONTROL CONSIDERATIONS

An information asset is any item of information providing material value to our organization. Information assets can be customer information, order information, trade secrets, recipes, architectural plans, intellectual property, or any of a huge number of other items of information. If we will feel an impact from the information going missing, being exposed to the public, being sold to hackers, and so on, this would be an indicator it was an information asset.

The important items to know when discussing information assets are what the assets are and how we go about protecting them. As with almost everything in the security industry, we need to have some understanding of a thing to be able to secure it. This can present a problem to us as security professionals, as no one has an inherent understanding of the value and impact of an information asset. Our information assets are handled by managers, engineers, developers, cooks, janitors, groundskeepers, and a large assortment of other people working in and around our environments on an everyday basis. If the person emptying the bins containing sensitive documents slated for shredding intermingles them with the regular recycling bin due to lack of understanding regarding the sensitivity of "just paper," then we might end up with a serious problem.

These and other potential issues we might wish to avoid can indicate the need to be careful in documenting the program and process pieces in place to prevent these sorts of incidents, as well as ensuring we take careful steps to train everyone who might have access to our information assets, all the way from the top down to the lowliest brook wielding janitor.

Administrative Controls

From an administrative standpoint, the controls around information assets will more often than not be based on policies and procedures. Our policies should be pointing out the high-level intent of how our information assets are to be handled, and the procedures should lend specific definition using the policies as a basis. From a policy perspective, we need to discuss the intent for protecting our information assets. Here we should be discussing the need to protect customer information, trade secrets, and the rest of the data on which our business depends. Having the appropriate procedures in place will help to protect us from incidents like our shred-bin-dumping janitor in the example we discussed earlier. These types of issues are so common they are often found as hot spots for investigation during various audits as well, so it would behoove us in a variety of ways to have these pieces of the program well road mapped out and be working toward implementation of them.

These controls, of course, will not stand by themselves and will fail if we do not communicate them and take steps to ensure our organization is trained in what we expect of them. We will discuss training and other similar needs in Chapter 8.

Technical Controls

Controlling the movement of information assets from a technical perspective can be a difficult task indeed. In the network-connected age in which we live, almost any device can connect to a network and store a file. This provides almost endless avenues for our information to move around in an unauthorized manner.

The set of technologies referred to as rights management is one possible solution to protecting, managing, and controlling access to our information assets. To boil down rights management technology into a bit of a simplified version of how it works we can use the example of a document containing sensitive data. We would like to be able to control how the document is used, who can access it, how many times it can be accessed and over what period of time, and whether it can be printed or edited, and we would like to be able to deny access to it, should it become necessary or desirable to do so. This sounds like an overwhelming set of things to keep track of for a single document, let alone a large set of them. To accomplish all of this, we can bring in a Rights Management System (RMS).

Rights Management

TIP

RMS systems are available from a number of vendors, including offerings from large companies such as Microsoft and Oracle. The amount of effort in implementing such a system can be large, but the security gains realized can be larger yet.

In essence, when we use the RMS, we encrypt our document in a special manner only the RMS can understand and decrypt. We then use a specific client to access the document. This might be a specific reader for the RMS or it might be a plugin for another tool, such as Microsoft Office. The client is configured to know where our back-end RMS servers are and how to talk to them, and it goes off and requests access to the document in the context of the user when we try to open it. The RMS server will check the specifics for the document and user to see what types of access are allowed and then relay this to the client. If the user is allowed to access the document and the document itself is still registered as being accessible, the user is provided access. This access might be further restricted by disallowing the user saving the document elsewhere or printing it, or any of a large number of other granular permissions.

Physical Controls

In addition to administrative and technical controls to protect our data, we also need to consider physical controls. Physical controls, i.e., those that prevent someone from just walking in and making off with the physical media on which our data are stored, may arguably be the most critical of the three control categories. If physical controls are not implemented, not implemented properly, or are subverted, then the technical and administrative controls may be nullified entirely. We will discuss physical controls in detail in the next section.

PHYSICAL AND ENVIRONMENTAL SECURITY FOR FACILITIES

In addition to the security of our personnel, when we look at security from a physical and environmental perspective, we have two major areas of concern: securing the area itself and securing the items within the area. To create a secure area from a physical perspective, we need to secure the site itself, using locks, guards, site layouts and landscaping, badges, video cameras, and so on. For the equipment within the facility, our security concerns become somewhat more environmental, i.e., providing stable power, keeping water where it belongs, and ensuring proper disposal of equipment. We also need to take into consideration the possibility of equipment or data storage devices leaving our facilities in an unauthorized manner.

Secure Areas

For site security we may see detective systems in the form of human or animal guards, whether they patrol an area on foot or monitor it secondhand through the use of technology such as camera systems. This type of monitoring has both good and bad points—a living being may be less focused than an electronic system, but does have the potential to become distracted and will need to be relieved for meals, bathroom breaks, and other similar activities. In addition, we can scale such guards from the lowliest unarmed security guard to well-armed security forces with a great deal of training, as is appropriate for the situation. As is true for most implementations involving security, the principle of defense in depth applies here.

When we discuss securing access to our equipment or our facility, we return again to the concept of defense in depth. There are multiple areas, inside and outside, where we may want to place a variety of security measures, depending on the environment. A military installation may have the highest level of security available, whereas a small retail store may have the lowest level.

We can often see measures for securing physical access implemented on the perimeter of the property on which various facilities sit. Often, we will at least see minimal measures in place to ensure vehicle traffic is controlled and does not enter undesirable places. Such measures may take the form of security landscaping. For example, we may see trees, large boulders, large cement planters, and the like placed in front of buildings or next to driveways to prevent unauthorized vehicle entry. At more secure facilities, we might see fences, concrete barriers, and other more obvious measures. Such controls are, in general, in place as deterrents, and may be preventive in nature as well.

At the facility itself, we should expect to see some variety of locks, whether mechanical or electronic with access badges, in place on the doors at the entrance to the building. A typical arrangement for nonpublic buildings is for the main entrance of the building to be unlocked during business hours and a security guard or receptionist stationed inside. In more secure facilities, almost all of the doors will be locked at all times, and a badge or key required to enter the building. Once inside the building, visitors will often have limited access to a lobby area, and, perhaps, meeting and restrooms, whereas those authorized to enter the rest of the building will use a key or badge to access it.

Once inside the facility, we will often see a variety of physical access controls, depending on the work and processes being carried out. We may see access controls on internal doors or individual floors of the building to keep visitors or unauthorized people from accessing the entire facility. Often, in the case where computer rooms or data centers are present, access to them will be restricted to those with a legitimate need to enter them for business reasons. We may also find more complex physical access controls in place in such areas, such as biometric systems.

Badges

Badges and the badge readers that accompany them are a physical control enabling us to restrict access to our employees, without having to deal with the distribution and relative irrevocability of having physical keys. Although badges do make a good control, they are not without their drawbacks.

Physical tailgating, also known as "piggybacking" is what most people think of when they hear the term used. This is the act of following someone through an access control point, such as secure door, without having the proper credentials, badge, or key, required to enter the door.

Tailgating is a problem endemic to locations that use technical access controls. In almost any location, unless strong steps have been taken to prevent it, we can see people tailgating. This is somewhat an issue of laziness, and somewhat an issue of the desire to avoid confrontation. In particular, in locations where the majority of foot traffic is composed of younger people, we will see tailgating policies flouted, i.e., closed school campuses, apartment buildings, etc., often in a willful fashion. Such locations make for easy tailgating targets.

A few tricks of equipment, such as knowing which props to use, and the use of psychology to allow attacker to play on the sympathies of others, will aid them in their tailgating efforts.

Video

Video monitoring can be a simple and, in relative terms, inexpensive method for adding a layer of security to a facility. Video monitoring systems can range from custom designed and installed systems in the tens or hundreds of thousands of dollars and represent the highest level of video and audio monitoring, to a canned system picked up from a big box store for a few hundred dollars and deployed in an hour or two. In either case, the systems provide similar functionality at a high level, in providing a deterrent to unwanted behavior when those under observation know they are present and monitored.

Video surveillance can also provide us with a historical record of the events within the range of its ability to monitor. This ability is, perhaps, even more important than the deterrent provided by the presence of the system as it gives us a foundation on which we can base investigations from a variety of angles. Although we might think the recording from the video surveillance system would be of use in the grossest of physical crimes, such is not the case at all. Records of physical movement throughout an area, or lack thereof, and the ability to track an individual's movement form one place to another, coupled with the time stamp often applied by video surveillance systems, can be invaluable in a great number of situations.

An additional step to take beyond video monitoring itself is the placement of signs in public places indicating video monitoring is in place. Video cameras are such a ubiquitous part of being in public or in a place of business these days they are nigh invisible in the background. The signs themselves do nothing to prevent people from acting in an undesirable fashion, but they do help to illustrate the idea there may be consequences for doing so and call attention to the fact there are cameras present. Such measures, while perhaps not contributing at a significant level to what we might think of as physical security, do help to keep honest people honest.

Equipment

Last on the list of our concerns for physical security, although still important and significant, is protecting our equipment, and, to a certain extent, the facilities housing it. This category falls last on the list because it represents the easiest and cheapest segment of our assets to replace. Even in case a major disaster destroys our facility and all the computing equipment inside it, as long as we still have the people needed to run our operation and are able to restore or access our critical data, we can be back in working order without a great deal of time elapsing. Replacing floor space or relocating to another area nearby can, in most cases, be accomplished with relative ease, and computing equipment is both cheap and plentiful. Although it may take us some time to be back to the same state we were in before the incident, getting to a bare minimum working state technology-wise is often a simple, if arduous, task.

Protecting Equipment

The physical threats harmful to our equipment, although fewer than those we might find harmful to people, are still numerous.

Extreme temperatures can be harmful to equipment. We often think of heat as being the most harmful to computing equipment, and this is correct for the most part. In environments with large numbers of computers and associated equipment, such as in a data center, we rely on environmental conditioning equipment to keep the temperature down to a reasonable level, often in the high 60s to mid-70s on the Fahrenheit scale, although there is some debate over the subject [1,2].

Liquids can be harmful to equipment, even when in quantities as small as those can be found in humid air. Depending on the liquid in question, and the quantity of it present, we may find corrosion in a variety of devices, short circuits in electrical equipment, and other harmful effects. In extreme cases, such as we might find in flooding, such equipment will often be rendered unusable after having been immersed.

Living organisms can also be harmful to equipment, although in the environments with which we will often be concerned, these will often be of the smaller persuasion. Insects and small animals gaining access to our equipment may cause electrical shorts, interfere with cooling fans, chew on wiring, and wreak all manner of havoc.

Movement in earth and in the structure of our facilities can be a bad thing for our equipment. One of the more obvious examples we can look at is an earthquake. Earthquakes can cause structural damage to our facilities, but the resultant shaking, vibrations, and potential for impacts due to structural failures can cause a large amount of damage.

Smoke and fire are bad for our equipment, as they introduce a number of harmful conditions. With smoke or fire, we might experience extreme temperatures, electrical issues, movement, liquids, and a variety of other problems. Efforts to extinguish fires, depending on the methods used, may also cause as much harm as the fire itself.

Utilities

In the case of security for utilities, our primary concern is electricity. Electrical anomalies can be harmful to any type of electrical equipment in a variety of ways. If we see issues with power being absent or not sending the expected amount of voltage, our equipment may be damaged beyond repair as a result. Good facility design will provide some measure of protection against such threats, but mitigating the effects of severe electrical issues, such as lightning strikes, can be difficult [3].

The best steps we can take to prepare ourselves for disruption of utilities are focused around disaster preparedness plans in place and tested well in advance of any incidents. In many larger organizations, such plans are covered under a set of policies and procedures referred to overall as business continuity planning and disaster recovery planning, often called BCP/DRP. BCP refers to the plans we put in place to ensure critical business functions can continue in a state of emergency. Disaster Recovery Plans (DRP) covers the plans we put in place in preparation for a potential disaster, and what we will do during and after a particular disaster strikes to get the technical infrastructure operational (often in a new location).

Disposal

As with many information security–related concepts, to secure something well we need to consider the various aspects of its life cycle. In the case of protecting equipment, we also need to see to its secure disposal. When we dispose of a server, desktop PC, phone, copier, controller for our air conditioning system, or almost anything containing electronics, we need to at least examine it to evaluate whether it contains anything sensitive and need data wiping or destruction before we dispose of it. We might look at something like a copier and assume it contained no sensitive data at all, but we might well be incorrect.

NOTE

In 2010, Affinity Health Plan returned a set of copiers to the leasing company from which they had come, with the assumption they contained no sensitive data. As later discovered by investigative journalists with CBS Evening News, information on 344,557 health care patients was contained on the devices [4], a breach of the Health Insurance Portability and Accountability Act (HIPAA) costing the company a hefty fine.

When we dispose of an item of equipment, we also need to keep a record of what was done to secure the device in question when it was decommissioned as well as a record of the serial and model numbers of the item for later reference.

ZONES OF TRUST AND CONTROL

Zones provide us a way of establishing areas of differing levels of security within our networks, to help mitigate risk and provide appropriate security controls within and at the perimeters of each of these areas. Zones are a network-centric implementation of the defense in depth concept.

Defense in depth is a strategy common to both military maneuvers and information security. In both senses, the basic concept of defense in depth is to formulate a multilayered defense that will allow us to still mount a successful defense should one or more of our defensive measures fail. In Fig. 6.1, we can see an example of the layers we might want to put in place to defend our assets from a logical perspective; we would at the very least want defenses at the external network, internal network, host, application, and data levels. Given well-implemented defenses at each layer, we will make it very difficult to successfully penetrate deeply into our network and attack our assets directly.

One important concept to note when planning a defensive strategy using defense in depth is that it is not a magic bullet. No matter how many layers we put in place, or how many defensive measures we place at each layer, we will

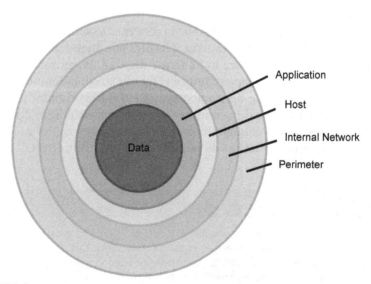

FIGURE 6.1
Defense in depth.

not be able to keep every attacker out for an indefinite period of time, nor is this the ultimate goal of defense in depth in an information security setting. The goal is to place enough defensive measures between our truly important assets and the attacker so that we will both notice that an attack is in progress and also buy ourselves enough time to take more active measures to prevent the attack from succeeding.

Security Zones

A security zone is an area of a network defined by a common set of security characteristics that define the systems that rest within it. A commonly recognized implementation of a security zone is what is referred to as a DMZ (demilitarized zone), which is a somewhat protected zone that has a greater level of protection than a device open on all ports to the Internet, but lesser than that of zones containing systems that have no need to be directly exposed to the Internet.

As we can see in Fig. 6.2, some of the more commonly implemented zones are:

- Untrusted—This zone is often used to categorize systems over which we have no control at all, such as those coming in from the open Internet.
- DMZ—This zone is used to house systems that require some level of exposure to the Internet, such as web servers, mail servers, File Transfer Protocol (FTP) servers, and so on.
- Trusted—This zone is often used for middleware servers that provide services to the servers in the DMZ, but do not house sensitive data.

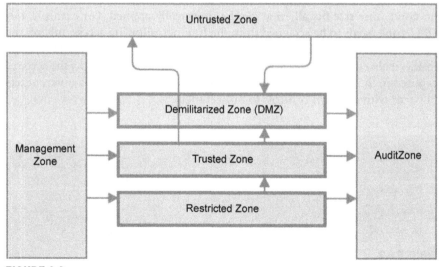

FIGURE 6.2
Zones.

- Restricted—The restricted zone, usually the most secure of all the zones, is where we will often find the sensitive data in an environment, such as credit card numbers or customer data. Data in the restricted zone will generally fall under one or more bodies of regulation governing how it is protected.
- Management—The management zone is used to provide access to the systems and people that manage the devices within all the other zones. Systems in the management zone can reach into the other zones, but this connectivity should only be in that direction.
- Audit—The audit zone is used to maintain audit data from all the other zones. Data flows into the audit zone from the other zones, but not in the other direction.

We may see other zones implemented in addition to the above-mentioned list of zones, as well as zones that have additional segmentation within. For example, we might see the Restricted Zone divided into further subzones, depending on the particular needs of the business and, perhaps, types of regulated data in the environment. The Restricted Zone might further be divided into subzones for PII, PCI, and HIPAA data, as shown in Fig. 6.3, each with its own set of controls and restrictions, as is appropriate for the type of data contained and the controls that need to be applied to it.

Implementing Zones

When implementing zones, we need to take into account the requirements for the zone in question and set up the appropriate controls to comply with these requirements. This will depend entirely on the needs of the zone, and there is no good "one size fits all" that can be universally applied. For example, our DMZ zone needs to be screened from the Internet, allowing access only on the ports needed to provide access to services that face the outside world. On the inside, it also needs to have access to the midtier systems that allow the services exposed in the DMZ to function properly. These are two relatively different sets of needs with different controls to protect them.

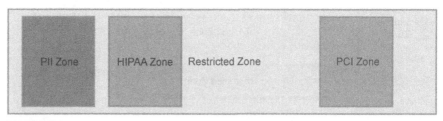

FIGURE 6.3

Subzones. *HIPAA*, Health Insurance Portability and Accountability Act; *PCI*, Payment Card Industry; *PII*, Personally Identifiable Information.

In general, we will likely use network segmentation, access control lists (ACLs), monitoring, and carefully limited zone interface points to control and protect zones and the boundaries in between them.

Network Segmentation

Network segmentation can go a long way toward reducing the impact of attacks. When we segment a network, we divide it into multiple smaller networks, each acting as its own small network called a subnet. We can control the flow of traffic between subnets, allowing or disallowing traffic based on a variety of factors, or even blocking the entire flow of traffic if necessary. Segmented networks can boost network performance by containing certain traffic only to the portions of the network needing to see it, and can help to localize technical network issues. In addition, network segmentation can prevent unauthorized network traffic or attacks from reaching portions of the network to which we would prefer to prevent access, as well as making the job of monitoring network traffic much easier.

Another design factor of assistance in the name of securing our networks is to funnel network traffic through certain points where we can inspect, filter, and control the traffic, often referred to as choke points. The choke points might be the routers moving traffic from one subnet to another; the firewalls or proxies controlling traffic moving within, into, or out of our networks or portions of our networks; or the application proxies filtering the traffic for particular applications such as Web or email traffic.

Access Between Zones

A key part of implementing security zones is being able to control access between them. When we have two zones of differing security levels, we do not want to make "Swiss cheese"-like access between them, as this would be difficult to both control and monitor. Instead, we want to carefully control how access is allowed between them and how many points there are at which traffic can move from one zone to the next. Additionally, traffic should not be able to skip zones, i.e., traffic going from the Restricted Zone to the DMZ must go through the intervening Trusted Zone, not straight from the Restricted Zone to the DMZ, as shown in Fig. 6.4.

Limiting Zone Interface Points

Access between zones should be limited to only a few interface points, as few as we can possibly get down to and have the ability to function as needed. This enables us to very carefully monitor and control these few choke points, as the scope of our monitoring and access controls is very small. When we open up a greater number of interface points between zones, this makes the task of controlling the movement between them considerably more difficult.

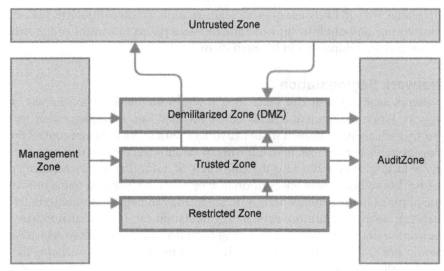

FIGURE 6.4
Zones.

Being able to limit interface points in this fashion, however, requires a certain amount of organization in our applications and environments. In the case where we have an application that is not cleanly divided up into application tiers, and/or we do not have cleanly segmented areas in which our data are centrally stored, this can be quite a task to bring order to in the fashion that we are discussing.

In many cases, regulatory compliance requirements will require us to limit zone interfaces in this fashion, at least to a certain extent. Speaking generically of regulated data, there is often a requirement that the data be stored in some central repository and that access to said repository be limited to the greatest possible extent. This is exactly the situation that we are setting up by putting zones in place and only allowing limited traffic between them.

Access Control Lists

When we look at the variety of activities that take place on networks, both private and public, we can again see ACLs regulating such activity. In the case of network ACLs, we typically see access controlled by the identifiers we use for network transactions, such as Internet Protocol (IP) addresses, Media Access Control (MAC) addresses, and ports. We can see such ACLs at work in network infrastructure such as routers, switches, and firewall devices, as well as in software firewalls, Facebook, Google, email, or other forms of software.

Permissions in network ACLs tend to be binary in nature, generally consisting of allow and deny. When we set up the ACL, we use our chosen identifier or identifiers to dictate which traffic we are referring to and simply state whether the traffic is to be allowed or not.

One of the simplest forms of network-oriented ACLs that we might see in place is MAC address filtering. MAC addresses are, in theory, unique identifiers attached to each network interface in a given system. Each network interface has a hard-coded MAC address issued when it is created.

We can also filter by the port being used to communicate over the network. Many common services and applications use specific ports to communicate over networks. For instance, FTP uses ports 20 and 21 to transfer files, Internet Message Access Protocol (IMAP) uses port 143 for managing email, Secure Shell uses port 22 to manage remote connections to systems, and many more—65,535 ports in all. We can control the use of many applications over the network by allowing or denying traffic originating from or sent to any ports that we care to manage. Like MAC and IP addresses, the specific ports that are used for applications are a convention, not an absolute rule. We can, with relative ease, change the ports that applications use to different ports entirely.

Using single attributes to construct ACLs is likely to present a variety of issues, including our attribute not being guaranteed to be unique, such as an IP address, or being easy to alter, such as a MAC address. When we use several attributes in combination we begin to arrive at a more secure technique. A very commonly used combination is that of IP address and port, typically referred to as a socket. In this way, we can allow or deny network traffic from one or more IP addresses using one or more applications on our network in a workable fashion.

We can also construct ACLs to filter on a wide variety of other things. In some cases, we might want to monitor the traffic going over our network to allow or deny traffic based on more specific criteria, such as the content of an individual packet or a related series of packets. Using such techniques, we can filter out traffic related to attacks, or traffic that is simply undesirable to us, such as that related to the peer-to-peer file-sharing networks commonly used to illegally share copyrighted songs, videos, and software.

Monitoring
Monitoring can provide us with an additional tool for managing the security of and within our zones. There are a variety of places that we can monitor and, in these places, specific items of data that we might be interested in.

Monitoring the flow of network traffic into, out of, and in between zones can be critical for maintaining security. In most cases there will be a desired directionality for the flow of data relative to our zones and, additionally, zones to which the flow of traffic is explicitly desired or not desired. For example, the PCI subzone of our Restricted Zone should only be seeing traffic to or from a very limited number of systems. If we see an unusual volume of traffic in comparison with the baseline for normal traffic flow, if we see traffic to hosts that normally do not communicate with the PCI subzone, or if we see a completely unusual traffic pattern, such as the PCI subzone exchanging traffic with the

Untrusted Zone, then we will have a very solid indicator that something has gone awry with our security controls and should immediately investigate.

We might also monitor the type or content of the data moving through our various zones. If we have a dedicated zone, for example, that should be the sole area for storage of sensitive data, then we might be on the lookout for this data in other parts of the environment where it should not be seen. If we were to find data containing large blocks of credit card numbers outside of our PCI subzone, then we would again have an indicator that something may have gone seriously wrong.

ENSURING DATA CONFIDENTIALITY

The use of cryptography is an integral part of computing, networking, and the vast set of transactions taking place over such devices on a regular basis. We use cryptography when we have conversations on our cell phones, check out email, buy things from online retailers, file our taxes, and do other activities. The chief security measure allowing us to make use of such technologies is cryptography—in the form of encryption. If we were not able to utilize encryption to protect the information we send over such channels, many of the Internet-based activities we enjoy today would be carried out at a much greater risk than they are carried out now.

To discuss cryptography it is helpful to first have a good understanding of the terms used to describe encryption, its components, and the people involved in its development and use.

Cryptography, practiced by cryptographers, is the science of keeping information secure. The term cryptography is, in everyday use, confused with encryption. Encryption itself is a subset of cryptography, referring to the transformation of unencrypted data, called plaintext or cleartext, into its encrypted form, called ciphertext. Decryption is the process of recovering the plaintext message from the ciphertext. The plaintext and ciphertext may also be referred to as the message.

The science of breaking through the encryption used to create the ciphertext is referred to as cryptanalysis and is practiced by cryptanalysts. The overarching field of study covering cryptography and cryptanalysis is referred to as cryptology and is practiced by cryptologists.

The specifics of the process used to encrypt the plaintext or decrypt the cyphertext is referred to as a cryptographic algorithm. Cryptographic algorithms use a key, or multiple keys, to encrypt or decrypt the message, this being, at a high level, analogous to a password. The range of all possible values for the key is referred to as the keyspace. We may also refer to the cryptosystem, a concept covering a given algorithm and all possible keys, plaintexts, and ciphertexts.

Cryptographic technologies depend on difficult mathematical problems, sometimes referred to as one-way problems. One-way problems are easy to perform in one direction but difficult to perform in the other direction. Factorization of large numbers is an example of a one-way problem. Such problems form the basis of many modern cryptographic systems.

Where We Use Encryption

We can divide practical uses of cryptography into three major categories: protecting data at rest, protecting data in motion, and protecting data in use. Protecting data at rest is important because of the large amount of stored data found on devices such as backup tapes, flash drives, and hard drives in portable devices such as laptops. Protecting data in motion is vital as well because of the enormous amount of business conducted over the Internet, including financial transactions, medical information, tax filings, and other sensitive exchanges. Last, protecting data while it is in use can be difficult, as we do need to allow access to the data at some point for it to have any utility at all.

In Motion

Another major concern to protecting our data comes when it is in motion over a network of some variety. This might be over a closed wide area network or local area network, over a wireless network, over the Internet, or in other ways. The primary method of securing data from exposure on network media is encryption, and we may choose to apply it in one of two main ways: by encrypting the data itself to protect it, or by protecting the entire connection.

We can take a variety of approaches to protect the data we are sending over the network, depending on what data we are sending and the protocols over which we are sending it.

Secure sockets layer (SSL) and transport layer security (TLS) are often used to protect information sent over networks and over the Internet, and they operate in conjunction with other protocols such as IMAP and Post Office Protocol for email, Hypertext Transfer Protocol for Web traffic, VoIP for voice conversations, instant messaging, and hundreds of others. SSL is the predecessor of TLS, and TLS is based on the last version of SSL. Both methods are still in common use.

Another approach we might choose to take is to encrypt all our network traffic with a virtual private network (VPN) connection. VPN connections use a variety of protocols to make a secure connection between two systems. We might use a VPN when we are connecting from an insecure network, such as the wireless connection in a hotel, to the internal resources secure behind our company firewalls.

At Rest

Protecting data at rest is an area in which security is often lax and is an area in which we choose not to emphasize security. Data are considered to be at rest when they are on a storage device of some kind and are not moving over a network, through a protocol, and so forth. Although it might sound somewhat illogical, data at rest on media can also be in motion; for example, we might ship a load of backup tapes containing sensitive data, carry in our pocket a flash drive containing a copy of our tax forms, or leave in the back seat of our car a laptop containing the contents of a customer database.

We can see this type of incident on a somewhat disturbing frequency basis in the media. In August 2013, the Advocate Medical Group in Park Ridge, Illinois, announced it had a breach of personal information due to the theft of four computers containing unencrypted storage media. The media contained sensitive information such as names, addresses, Social Security numbers, and dates of birth of more than 4 million patients [5]. Had the group taken the necessary steps to protect its data at rest by encrypting it, not only would it have not had such a large security incident, but it also may have been spared from having to disclose the incident had occurred, thus saving quite a bit of embarrassment [6].

At Use

The last category of protecting data involves securing them while they is being used. Although we can use encryption to protect data while they are stored or moving across a network, we are somewhat limited in our ability to protect data while they are being used by those who have legitimate access to it. Authorized users can print files, move them to other machines or storage devices, email them, share them on peer-to-peer (P2P) file-sharing networks, and make a mockery of our care laid security measures.

In June of 2013, it was discovered classified information containing details on the US National Security Agency PRISM program, designed to collect and review terrorism-related communications flowing through, in, and out of the United States, had been leaked to news agencies by a government contractor named Edward Snowden [5,7]. This is a case of sensitive data being lost, but we can also see many examples of companies holding and working with data sensitive to businesses and individuals on a regular basis.

MAKING USE OF TESTED TECHNOLOGIES

In the information technology field in general, but particularly in the area of information security, it is very important to make use of technologies that have been tried and tested. For security-focused technologies, algorithms, controls of various kinds, and a wide variety of other items that serve the goal of information security, it is critical that we use technologies that have been subjected to careful scrutiny before being released for public use.

In many cases, it is a relatively small set of architects, designers, and developers who are involved in putting a security product together. This product will then often be implemented in places where it is subject to the tender ministrations of a vast multitude of attackers, security researchers, inept users, trolls, and other such horrors. The product will be poked, prodded, abused, and used in ways that those designing it never intended, and it must be able to withstand all of this without failing in its primary task of providing security.

Customization

Customization in security solutions, even in the case of existing and well-known technologies, can lead to issues as well. This is not to say that we should stick to the stock implementation of the tool or solution in question and should not configure it to meet the needs of our environment, but that we should not alter it beyond the point of being supportable by our staff and the vendor of the tool, and should not make heroic efforts to make the tool do things that it was never intended to do. It is all too tempting to make use of Application Program Interfaces (APIs), scriptable extensions, direct access to database back ends of products, and other similar "under-the-hood" features to make a product jump through hoops.

The happy medium here is to customize our security solutions to the point where they fit our needs, as can be done within the reasonable and supportable bounds of the product, service, or solution. If we take the "my only tool is a hammer" approach and attempt to stretch a product to cover an area for which it was not intended to serve, then we are only going to cause ourselves, or those who come after us, future pain. This goes double for crafting entirely custom solutions for complex problems.

Although it is admirable, cost-effective, and an efficient use of resources to script out or code a solution to solve an administrative issue or automate a repetitive task, there are bounds within which this is reasonable. We can expect to be successful in putting together a tool to manage a task such as putting together a bash or Powershell script to handle deploying a vendor-provided full disk encryption tool to a fleet of laptops. We are much less likely to succeed if we also attempt to develop the encryption product itself using Powershell as well. Where exactly the bounds are for what is and is not reasonable in this area is a judgment call.

Why Developing Your Own Encryption Is a Bad Idea

In addition to what we have already discussed about the security benefits of using tested technologies and why excessive customization can cause security and a variety of other issues, building custom encryption technologies is a special case. Building encryption algorithms and the hardware and/or software tools that make use of them is a very difficult task. Cryptography is actually one of the fields that make use of very advanced math and a cryptographic tool is a conjunction of said very advanced math and a relatively fragile set of code and hardware to support it. The smallest mistake in development or implementation can render the entire set of protections null and enable attackers to effortlessly glide past the control.

As an example of this, we can look to the flawed encryption used by the Open Smart Grid Protocol (OSGP), primarily used in smart meters for electrical utilities. The OSGP "is optimized to provide reliable and efficient delivery of command and control information for smart meters, direct load control modules, solar panels, gateways, and other smart grid devices" [8]. The crux of the issue, and there are many, with encryption in OSGP is the OMA Digest Message Authentication Code (MAC). Several of these issues are described in detail in the papers Dumb Crypto in Smart Grids: Practical Cryptanalysis of the Open Smart Grid Protocol [9] and Structural Weaknesses in the Open Smart Grid Protocol [10], and more were uncovered by a variety of security researchers probing the protocol for further weaknesses.

It can be very tempting to create a custom encryption tool, but, as with the OSGP example, doing so may lead to considerable rework when flaws with the system are discovered down the road. Using carefully developed and tested cryptographic tools does not always guarantee a happy result either, but at least such tools will have been carefully vetted and simple flaws such as those discussed earlier are much more likely to have already been discovered and remediated.

ACTIONS

Classify data and assign sensitivity and criticality

- All data in the environment need to be assigned levels of sensitivity and criticality. A system and accompanying processes need to be developed to maintain data classification and controls must exist to manage data in accordance with it.

Decide how to implement confidentiality

- Confidentiality is generally implemented through encryption. Determine what type of encryption is appropriate for the situation and what algorithm(s) will be used.

Develop an access control program

- Develop a program for limiting access to resources in the environment. This should be based on the principle of least privilege.

Develop requirements for physical and environmental security

- Based on the organizational risk appetite, develop requirements for physical and environmental security.

Decide on controls for physical and environmental security

- Based on the stated requirements, select controls for physical and environmental security.

Develop architectural zones of trust and control.

- Based on good security practices and the requirements driven by any regulated data present in the environment, develop zones of trust and control.

Use existing security technologies

- To make use of the most thoroughly tested security technologies and avoid overcustomization, avoid implementing custom or one-off security controls.

References

[1] Juvenal VI. [Internet]. Available: http://www.thelatinlibrary.com/juvenal/6.shtml.

[2] The data center temperature debate | Data Center Knowledge. In: Data Center Knowledge [Internet]. June 07, 2010. Available: http://www.datacenterknowledge.com/archives/2010/06/07/the-data-center-temperature-debate/.

[3] Frequently asked questions about Cybersecurity and the Electric Power Industry [Internet]. Available: http://www.eei.org/issuesandpolicy/cybersecurity/documents/cybersecurity_faq.pdf.

[4] $1.2 million penalty in Copier Breach [Internet]. Available: http://www.databreachtoday.com/12-million-penalty-in-copier-breach-a-5991.

[5] Personal data of 4M patients at risk after Advocate breakin. In: Tribunedigital-chicagotribune [Internet]. Available: http://articles.chicagotribune.com/2013-08-23/business/chi-advocate-health-break-in-20130823_1_credit-report-advocate-medical-group-advocate-health-care.

[6] OCR Hitech Breach Notification Interim Final Rule. U.S. Department of Health and Human Services. 2009. Available: http://www.hhs.gov/.

[7] Greenwald G, MacAskill E, Poitras L. Edward Snowden: the whistleblower behind the NSA surveillance revelations. In: The Guardian [Internet]. June 11, 2013. Available: http://www.theguardian.com/world/2013/jun/09/edward-snowden-nsa-whistleblower-surveillance.

[8] What is OSGP? – OSGP Alliance. In: OSGP Alliance [Internet]. Available: http://www.osgp.org/what-is-osgp/.

[9] Dumb Crypto in Smart Grids: Practical Cryptanalysis of the Open Smart Grid Protocol [Internet]. Available: https://eprint.iacr.org/2015/428.pdf.

[10] Structural Weaknesses in the Open Smart Grid Protocol [Internet]. Available: https://eprint.iacr.org/2015/088.pdf.

CHAPTER 7

Manage the Security of Third Parties and Vendors

THIRD PARTY AGREEMENTS

When we are looking to third party agreements, there are a couple of major areas of concern: regulatory agreements and security agreements. Regulatory agreements are the general container for issues specific to regulated data and working through a third party and security agreements are the general set of agreements between us and a third party to ensure that strong security is upheld. We will talk about both areas.

Regulatory Agreements

In the realm of the regulatory agreements under which we are bound to operate, we must also ensure that any third parties that we have engaged in handling such data, whether storing, transmitting, or processing, are compliant as well. This can be a tricky area with a third party, as the particulars of what exactly needs to happen must be very carefully spelled out.

Defining Sensitive Data

When we are working with a third party and sensitive or potentially sensitive data, we need to very carefully define what exactly it is that is sensitive, for what reason, and within what parameters.

In a general sense, sensitive data might include:

- ethnicity or race
- religious preference
- sexual preference
- health details, both physical and mental
- legal or criminal history
- full name and/or relative's names
- address of residence
- mailing address
- Social Security number
- date of birth
- biometric details—hair color, eye color, height, weight

125

Building a Practical Information Security Program. http://dx.doi.org/10.1016/B978-0-12-802042-5.00008-1

- phone number
- IP address
- MAC address

And a dizzying array of other such details. Even within the bounds of an organization, it can be difficult to say what are and are not sensitive data and how any given item of data needs to be protected. When we are dealing with a third party, we need to be very explicit about this information. Ultimately, we need to very carefully document what we expect of the third party in great detail of we expect them to behave in a particular fashion.

Breach Notifications

When working with third parties, we need to be very clear on expectations and requirements for notifications from them in the event of a breach. Typically, even if a vendor is not directly the cause of a breach, for example, if a payment card processor were to suffer a breach and allow unauthorized access to credit card transaction information from a particular vendor, it is the primary vendor, not the third party, that will end up notifying customers of the issue.

The major concern is the rules and, perhaps even more so important, the contractual language, that governs the third party requirements to report breaches that might be of concern to us. In the case of a significant breach, we may need to take immediate steps to remediate the issue within our own environments by changing credentials, reissuing payment cards, and so on.

Unfortunately, in many cases, breaches are not reported on while they are being actively investigated. If it was the case that this had happened, we could be continuing to incur damages and not even know that anything untoward was taking place.

Industry-Specific Issues

Industry-specific issues, again, may have some overlap with the categories that we have already discussed earlier, and more as well. Although the particular categories of data may not be changed, the emphasis placed on them may be much stronger in some areas. For example, let us look briefly at the retail and education industries.

Retail

In the retail industry, most of the concern revolves around the protection of payment card data in (hopefully) segmented portions of the environment known as the cardholder data environment (CDE) [1]. In the case that we are working with third parties, much of the concern will be around making sure that they do not have unauthorized access to the CDE, and that the CDE is appropriately segmented from the systems that they control.

This is a lesson that Target learned the hard way, as the root cause of its 2014 breach was attackers gaining access through an improperly segmented heating, ventilation, and air conditioning system directly from the internet [2].

Education

In the education world, the focus is on protecting students and the data that relate to them. Among a variety of administrative controls, rules, and regulations that help to manage the protection of student data in general, we also have technical controls in place, similar in a general nature to those for payment or healthcare data. In the same sense, educational data must be segmented and appropriately secured when stored, in motion, or in use.

Given the stringent federal regulations around educational data, we must be very careful when working with third parties that may have any level of access to it.

Security Agreements

The security agreements that we put in place with our vendors define how we expect them to behave from an information security perspective. Some of the main areas that we may want to look at are information security agreements, privacy agreements, auditing and monitoring agreements, and foreign corrupt practices agreements.

Information Security Agreement

Our information security agreements with third parties are designed to communicate to them what our minimum standards are for information security and what practices we expect them to follow. These practices, just as our own, are designed to ensure the security of our data, our customer data, and our information assets in general.

Such agreements are generally built around a security framework of some kind, frequently the ISO 27002 control categories:

- Information security policies
- Organization of information security
- Human resource security
- Asset management
- Access control
- Cryptography
- Physical and environmental security
- Operation security—procedures and responsibilities, protection from malware, backup, logging and monitoring, control of operational software, technical vulnerability management, and information systems audit coordination

- Communication security—network security management and information transfer
- System acquisition, development, and maintenance—security requirements of information systems, security in development and support processes, and test data
- Supplier relationships—information security in supplier relationships and supplier service delivery management
- Information security incident management—management of information security incidents and improvements
- Information security aspects of business continuity management—information security continuity and redundancies
- Compliance—compliance with legal and contractual requirements and information security reviews

ISO 27002 may not be the perfect fit for every environment, but it is a good starting place. There are a number of other similar frameworks that may work equally as well in a given case.

Information Privacy Agreement

The agreements that we have in place with third parties to protect the privacy and confidentiality of our data are highly important in the set of agreements that we have with our business associates. We should note that it is a very common practice in the business world to share data among companies in the same industry, owned by the same parent companies, other business partners, and so on, with a relative degree of freedom. If we do not wish our data to be shared on such a basis, we need to explicitly build this into our contract language so that our intentions are clear.

Additionally, we need to be very clear about the international use of our data. In many cases, laws regarding the handling of data vary heavily from one country to another. What is a completely unproblematic set of data to collect, process, and store in one country may be the start of an international incident in another. If we have restrictions on where data may or may not travel geographically, we need to build this into our third party agreements.

Auditing and Monitoring Agreement

When working with third parties, we need to provide clear responsibility for the security of our data at all levels of management, both within our own organization and within the third party. Just as is the case within our own organization, if we do not clearly communicate our expectations, we should not be surprised when they are not met.

We also need to understand what exactly the culture of security is within the organizations that we have third party relationships with. We should be seeing evidence of security training for new hires and also evidence of ongoing security education and awareness efforts. Additionally, we need to see evidence that new hires are being carefully vetted before they are allowed to handle data of a sensitive nature.

We need to ensure vendors have placed controls around our sensitive data being handled by our third party relationships, such as the monitoring, incident response, use of encryption, data loss prevention tools, system hardening, segmentation, and so on. If at any point unusual activity is discovered, we need to take swift action to ensure that issues are resolved.

Foreign Corrupt Practices Agreement

The Foreign Corrupt Practices Act of 1977 (FCPA) is primarily concerned with transparency as pertains to the Securities and Exchange Commission and the bribery of anyone through personal payments, gifts, etc. Companies can also be held liable for the actions of third parties under the FCPA. This is primarily done to keep companies from acting through other companies to escape the results of their actions.

When working with third parties, we need to carefully monitor for anything that might be criminal activity and take immediate action on it if such practices are found. If our organization is found to have had knowledge of any such activities, or to have been "willfully blind" to them, we may be held responsible for resulting issues. We need to put processes in place to monitor and audit the activities of our third party relationships so that we can detect any abnormalities that might indicate unusual discounting, price changes, or other such activities that might be used to cover up bribery.

ENSURING COMPLIANCE

In our agreements with third parties, we need to work diligently to ensure that they are maintaining compliance with both what we have directly agreed between us when developing the relationship with the other organization, as well as the regulatory requirements that both organizations are bound by. We can do this through the risk assessment mechanism, as well as various enforcement mechanisms that we may choose to use.

Risk Assessment

In our third party relationships, just as within our own organizations, we can use risk assessments to help surface some of the issues that we may run into later and deal with them before they become much larger problems. There are a few areas in which we may want to specifically focus our risk management efforts as pertaining to external organizations:

- network connectivity
- data handling

- data destruction
- employment practices
- physical security

Network connectivity can be a particularly sensitive area when it comes to allowing others to connect to our infrastructure. Whether this is indirect through the use of applications, or a site-to-site virtual private network connection, there is risk involved and we must ensure that any outside entities are appropriately restricted in terms of access, segmented off from areas that they do not need access to, and monitored appropriately.

Data handling is an enormous issue when we are sharing data with outside organizations. The potential for such efforts to work out in an undesirable fashion can be very large, particularly when we are working with sensitive data or regulated data. We need to carefully put controls in place to ensure that our data are protected in use, in motion, and at rest.

Data destruction is at least equally important to protect as data handling is. If our data are not disposed of properly, we may very well end up on the news due a box of printer out customer data being found in a dumpster. All of our data should be carefully controlled, and disposed of in a secure and certified manner, which is then reported back to us on a regular basis.

The employment practices of third parties should also be of great concern to us. If the other organization is not carefully screening new potential hires, as well as background checking them, conducting credit inquiries, drug testing, etc., then we have no idea who it is that will be handling our data. We should expect a hiring standard from third parties to be at least as strong as our own. In the case where those being hired are overseas, we need to be even more careful. The differing laws in other countries as relates to hiring, personal data, and any other such HR-related issues are an area in which we should tread very carefully.

Physical security is also an area in which we need to take great care. An old saw of information security is that it is "game over" if we lose the ability to control the physical security of the environment in which our information assets are housed. We should carefully review the physical environments of our third party associates to ensure that they are adequately constructed. In particular, if we are in a situation where the third party has direct network connectivity to use, we might find ourselves in a situation where their physical compromise results in a situation where attackers are able to bypass our network security entirely though something as simple as social engineering.

Enforcement Mechanisms

There are a number of mechanisms that we can use as part of our efforts to enforce compliance in third party relationships. Among them are auditing and monitoring, oversight, reporting, third party reviews, and, if need be, termination.

Auditing and Monitoring

Once our business relationship has been established, we need to perform ongoing monitoring to be sure of our ability to manage the risks around working closely with another organization. Just as we would with our internal risk assessments, we need to be aware of changes in the environment, processes, technologies used, and any of a number of other such factors.

In general, we will want to perform audits on a cyclical basis, once per year being a common interval for this. We may elect to conduct such audits ourselves, or we may decide to outsource this function to an external partner that specializes in such functions. We will discuss the use of external auditors later in this section.

We may also want to build performance measurements in our contracts with third parties. This gives us a solid baseline to measure compliance against when we are auditing and gives the third party organization a clear set of goals that they need to accomplish, as well as a way of reporting associated risks within our own organization. As with many contractual stipulations, there may also be penalties specified with noncompliance on the third party's end.

Third Party Reviews

Third party reviews give us the opportunity to have a consistent and unbiased review that will give us solid evidence as to whether our business partners are behaving in the manner that we expect them to. Such reviews are typically conducted on an annual basis and there are many consulting companies that are willing and able to conduct such reviews around the globe. Some of the more common types of standardized reviews might include:

- PCI DSS (Payment card industry data security standard) certification
- ISO 27002 certification
- OWASP (Open web application security project) Application Security Verification Standard certification
- SAS (Statement on auditing standards) 70 Type II
- SSAE-16 (Statement on standards for attestation engagements)
- Verizon Cybertrust
- SOC (Service organization controls) 1,2,&3

Although none of these is the proverbial "magic bullet" that will guarantee the absolute security, they do provide us with a certain level of baseline for how the organization being evaluated handles information security and risk management within their environments. In many cases, one or more of these reviews are considered to be the minimum bar to conduct business in certain industries.

Reporting

Properly documenting and reporting the state of our third party relationships enables oversight, monitoring, and risk management in general. Such documentation and associated reporting is typically metrics driven, some of which might include:

- degree of compliance with security requirements
- number of incidents
- incident resolution rate and time
- organizational financial condition
- insurance coverage
- service level agreement compliance

As with similar discussions we have had throughout this book regarding metrics, we will typically roll these up into a set of key performance indicators to report performance in broad categories across all of our third party relationships. Typically such reporting is done at an executive management or board level to enable these levels of management to develop and update our organizational strategy as relates to our third party business partners.

Termination

As a last resort, we should develop a plan and contingencies for transitioning away from the third party relationship in which we are involved. This may happen through breach of contract, failure to satisfy the terms of the contract, contracts ending, organizational changes on one side or the other, or any of a number of such occurrences.

We should have several plans for this eventuality, potentially including bringing the functions back in-house, transferring them to a different third party, changing the processes being used entirely, and so on. This is an area in which we should plan both carefully and in advance. If we have not done so, we may find ourselves locked into a relationship by a particular issue, for example, simply for lacking the technical means or resources to move from one environment to another. Cloud services can be particularly tricky in this regard.

ACTIONS

Evaluate agreements with managed services

- Carefully evaluate all managed service agreements to ensure that they are consistent with our expected security posture

Develop governance program for managed services

- Ensure that a proper set of policies and processes exists to keep managed services functioning within the expected bounds and roles

Establish contractor agreements

- Define regulatory requirements as relates to the contract agency
- Put security agreements in place to ensure an acceptable level of information security efforts on the part of the contract agency

Establish third party agreements

- Define regulatory requirements as relates to the third party
- Put security agreements in place to ensure an acceptable level of information security efforts on the part of the third party

Ensure third party compliance

- Conduct risk assessment to determine risks associated with third party business partners
- Put enforcement mechanisms in place to ensure ongoing compliance

References

[1] [No title] [Internet]. Available: https://www.pcisecuritystandards.org/pdfs/pci_dss_glossary_v1-1.pdfhttps://www.pcisecuritystandards.org/pdfs/pci_dss_glossary_v1-1.pdf.

[2] Target Hackers Broke in Via HVAC Company — Krebs on Security [Internet]. Available: http://krebsonsecurity.com/2014/02/target-hackers-broke-in-via-hvac-company/http://krebsonsecurity.com/2014/02/target-hackers-broke-in-via-hvac-company/.

Conduct Security Awareness and Training

PARTNERING WITH STAKEHOLDERS

To successfully launch and maintain a security awareness and training program, we need to partner with the stakeholders that have an interest in seeing such a program succeed. If we do not have support of the right stakeholders, we are very likely to fail in our efforts. Security awareness and training are a critical part of the information security program and such efforts need to be carefully planned, socialized, and supported if they are to be of any effect.

Who Are the Stakeholders for Security Training?

Although the specific stakeholders for our security awareness and training program are very likely to vary from one organization to the next, there are several categories of people that we will commonly see represented. From the top down, stakeholders generally include our board of directors, senior management, management, and employees. Let us look at each of these groups and talk about why they have a stake in our security awareness and training program.

Board of Directors

The board has a fiduciary responsibility to represent and protect the interests of the employees, investors, and customers. The board is one of the main, if not the main stakeholder in properly training those that work for the organization on how to behave in a secure manner. As the board is responsible for protecting the assets of the company, it is ultimately and directly responsible for security issues that occur.

135

Building a Practical Information Security Program. http://dx.doi.org/10.1016/B978-0-12-802042-5.00009-3

In some cases, members of the board and/or executives may even be held personally responsible in the case of particularly egregious breach or incident. In 2014 during the Palkon v. Holmes case, a shareholder of Wyndham Worldwide Corporation directly sued members of Wyndam's board, claiming failure to implement strong enough information security policies enabled repeated data breaches and large losses of customer data [1].

Security training can benefit the board in several ways. Perhaps in one of the most obvious ways, it can help to prevent the members of the board from being held personally responsible for incidents that occur. Of course, having a security awareness and training program will not directly prevent such incidents from taking place, but properly trained users are much less likely to unknowingly cause such incidents to take place because of lack of training that told them what the security behavior expected of them actually was. We should also consider security training for the members of the board directly. As they are dealing with some of the most sensitive data that can be found in the organization, from a strategic perspective, they should not be overlooked in our efforts.

Secure practices, to a certain extent, as part and parcel of our awareness and training program can also help to drive business to the organization. Particularly in case where sensitive data are being handled by the company, customers and business partners will often want to know some level of detail regarding how their data are protected. Particularly in the wake of several years of major data breaches from large public companies like Target and Home Depot the need for sound security practices is much more in the public eye. We might very well find that customers and business partners are willing to seek out other business opportunities if our organization is unable to demonstrate that it has some level of commitment to sound security practices.

Management

Management, including all management from officers of the company to project managers, has a vested interest in a strong information security program being in place.

Management needs to be informed about security risks to critical assets and what the potential impacts of these might be, as well as the current state asset protection and legal and regulatory compliance. For all or any of this to happen successfully, we need to have a well-educated security staff, an end point that is reached through the implementation and execution of a security awareness and training program that includes and supports providing the required information.

The members of management are also responsible for ensuring that the company succeeds in its aims and goals and part of this effort is making sure that the assets of the company are secure.

Security awareness and training benefit management in two major ways. Such programs help to ensure that the organization and its assets are secure, and they also help to ensure that incidents are handled in an appropriate manner.

Keeping the organization's assets secure is an effort that spans the entire company. From management to engineering and development, down to the lowliest admin maintaining the email server starting their first day on the job, information security hinges on every person making security decisions as they move through their day and carry out the tasks that are required of them. A large portion of making sure that this happens in the way that we would like to is to support the security programs that help to ensure behavior trending in the direction that we would like.

Secondly, management would like us to handle incidents in an appropriate manner. We would expect the incident response team to be well trained in how to specifically respond to an incident, but this team will likely not be the very first team on the scene in many cases. We also need those who detect and report the issue or work in the vicinity of the equipment involved with it to behave securely. As these behaviors, at least in terms of incidents, involve not following the natural inclination to start digging into the problem, this is definitely an area in which specific training is required for a large set of personnel.

Individual Contributors

As we have discussed repeatedly in the last several sections, we expect quite a lot out of individual contributors in terms of security behaviors. We expect them to safeguard data when they are of a sensitive nature, to report incidents appropriately but not interfere to the extent of causing issues for those who will be investigating later, and numerous other security bits and pieces. For those who are not in information security or information technology (IT), this can be a daunting set of tasks, some of which may seem nonsensical or even counterintuitive. Individual contributors definitely have a stake in how the security awareness and training program is constructed and carried out, as they are ultimately the end audience for what is produced.

Individual contributors can provide us with a considerable amount of feedback as we put our awareness program together. From the standpoint of information security, much as is the case of any other specialized field inside or outside of technology, many of these policies and processes seem to make inherent sense to us. We are surprised when people make decisions that do not parallel what we expect for user behavior. Unfortunately, this is not a reasonable expectation without training.

Security awareness and training benefit individual contributors by giving them a definition for what we expect them to do, how we expect them to do it, and under what circumstances they should be doing what. Such items should be based on our security processes and policies. Without defining the rules of the game for them, we cannot very well expect them to play it properly, if at all. If we can carefully define what we expect of them, we will all be considerably more successful.

TARGETING TRAINING NEEDS FOR THE AUDIENCE

When we conduct security awareness and training, we need to be careful to tailor it to the various audiences that we will be interfacing with. If we do not do so, we will likely experience issues in communication and render the training considerably less effective by delivering overly technical content to nontechnically savvy audiences and information at too high of a level to technical audiences. There is no such thing as a one-size-fits-all security training program that will be effective for all audiences. In broad categories, we will need to customize our training for the general audience, various technical staff, and management. We are more likely to carry this out in a successful manner by developing a general training that can be delivered to everyone, then providing additional training for those who need specialized content.

Training for All Staff

When we produce training intended for all of our staff, we should be careful to use less technical jargon and detail and put more emphasis on explaining things in relatable terms. The typical set of topics for such training might include:

- passwords
- internet usage
- social engineering
- malware
- social media
- sensitive data
- information security policies

We will briefly look at each of these areas and the typical items that are covered.

Passwords

- Do not write passwords down—Users should understand the dangers of recording passwords in an insecure manner.
- Do not share passwords—Users should understand that their login credentials are specifically attached to them as individuals.
- Do not create passwords from personal information—Users should understand that password created from personal information can be easily guessed by attackers who have researched them to find such details.
- Use strong passwords (pass-phrases)—Users should understand why constructing a strong password renders it more difficult for attackers to guess or brute force.
- Choose password reset questions carefully—Users should understand why choosing weak answers or basing them on easily found information makes reset questions dangerous.

Internet Usage

- Do not use personal equipment on the corporate network—Users should understand why putting personal or vendor equipment on the corporate network can be dangerous.
- Monitoring—Users should understand that their activities on the corporate network are monitored and what expectations, if any, they have for privacy.
- Beware of suspicious sites, popups, and activity—Users should understand that they should be aware of and report suspicious activity on the computer systems that they use.
- Do not send sensitive information unprotected—Users should understand what appropriate and inappropriate ways of handling sensitive data are.
- Working away from the office—Users should understand how to safely work with corporate data and systems when remote.

Social Engineering

- Phishing, spear phishing—Users should understand what phishing and spear phishing attacks are and how they can be identified.
- Different types of phishing attacks—Users should be able to identify phishing attacks via email, SMS, social media, and phone.
- Building access by strangers—Users should understand their responsibility for ensuring that unauthorized or unusual people in corporate facilities are reported.
- Tailgating—Users should understand what tailgating is and how it can be used by attackers.

Malware

- What malware is—Users should understand, at a high level, what forms malware can take and how they might recognize it.
- Protective tools in place—Users should understand what tools are in place in the environment to protect them from malware and what they look like when running and alerting.
- Email and attachments—Users should understand how malware can use email attachments as an attack vector and how they can recognize suspicious or abnormal email and attachments.
- Shortened URLs—Users should understand why shortened URLs can be dangerous and what tools they might use to see what address a shortened URL leads to.

Social Media

- Favorite of attackers—Users should understand why social media sites and applications are a favorite tool of attackers.
- Think before posting—Users should understand the dangers of posting sensitive and personal data to social media.

- Social media as a vehicle for attacks—Users should understand how social media can be used for phishing, malware, and password stealing attacks.
- Social media at work—Users should understand the circumstances under which social media is and is not acceptable to use in the workplace.

Sensitive Data

- Sensitive data—Users should understand what constitutes sensitive data in their environment and what the requirements are for handling it.
- Internal use—Users should understand what constitutes internal use data in their environment and what the requirements are for handling it.
- Public—Users should understand what constitutes public data in their environment and under what conditions such data are shared with the public.

Information Security Policies

- What the main information security policies are—Users should understand what the main information security policies are and be familiar with them at a high level.
- Where the policies can be found—Users should understand where policies in general can be found and specifically where to go to find the information security policies.
- Periodic policy review and acknowledgment—Users should understand what their responsibilities are as related to the requirements for periodic review and acknowledgement of the information security policies.

Additional Training for Technical Staff

When we are training technical staff, we will cover, at some level, the same items as we will for all staff, but at a greater level of detail and with more technical explanations. In addition to these items, we will also cover areas that relate to their specific area of responsibility in technology. Typically this means additional training for IT staff and for developers. This audience has greater access and needs role-based training to understand the risks they take by simple acts like using their admin login for everyday access.

Information Technology Staff

Our IT staff will often be exposed to security-related situations and incidents, will have a greater level of exposure to sensitive data, and will be responsible for maintaining the infrastructure on which the organization runs. Given these responsibilities, this staff will need additional training so that they know how they are expected to handle these responsibilities and accesses.

Incident Reporting and Response

Even if they are not directly part of the information security team, IT staff will often be in a position that exposes them to security-related situations or incidents. The IT staff should understand how to handle these situations properly, including whom they should call or notify if they think an incident might be occurring, how they should respond directly they are responsible for doing so, and so on. In many cases, staff responding improperly to an incident can make the situation considerably worse for doing so. At the very least, they should know where to go to look up the process or procedure that defines how they should respond to a given situation.

Data Protection

IT staff should understand what their responsibilities are in the area of data protection. Given their position, they will likely be exposed to a variety of sensitive or regulated data, perhaps bound by a variety of international laws on top of whatever regulatory requirements exist. Given the potentially very complex web of requirements for protecting such data, we should ensure that our expectations are carefully defined for how these situations should be handled. For those working specifically with regulated data such as that governed by Payment Card Industry (PCI) or Health Insurance Portability and Accountability Act (HIPAA), training specific to these areas may be needed or required.

Environmental Security

IT staff will often be responsible for maintaining the security of the environment. They should understand what is required of them for typical IT activities such as installing patches, updating software, creating backups, onboarding and off boarding users, securely installing equipment, disposing of equipment and media, or any of a number of other similar tasks for which the IT staff is responsible on a daily basis. This can be one of the broadest and most critical areas for training as a poorly or insecurely maintained environment can be the cause for an innumerable amount of issues further down the road.

Software Development

Software developers and software engineers are in a position to greatly help or harm the overall security posture of the products for which they are responsible. In many cases, the reputation of the organization in general can suffer grave damage if the products that it produces develop a reputation for being insecure. Adobe, a company much maligned for producing products with a wide variety of security flaws has had many issues with exactly this situation over the years and has taken steps such as renaming its particularly security bug-stricken Flash product, a move though by some to be designed to shed some of the damaged confidence in the process [2].

Secure Software Development

Although it might seem like developing software in a secure manner would be relatively simple and intuitive, this is anything but the case. Developing software securely is a very difficult task, exacerbated by the fact that each language has some set of different problem areas on top of the common areas that plague all programming languages. For a developer to code securely in a new language they need to understand the security peculiarities of that language and what needs to be done to work around them. In short, each language that we are working with in our development efforts will require at least some additional training for our developers to write security code in it.

Vulnerabilities

Although there are a wide variety of potential software vulnerabilities, most of them fall into a few main categories [3]:

- buffer overflows
- invalidated input
- race conditions
- access-control problems
- weaknesses in authentication, authorization, or cryptographic practices

Although this information is useful at a high level, developers need to be able to recognize these types of vulnerabilities and understand what the impact of them is in the software that they are developing. Although part of this equation comes with security software development training, a solid understanding of specifically why these sets of vulnerabilities are problematic can be invaluable.

TIP

The OWASP (open web application security project) top 10 list,[1] although specific to web applications, can be of great utility for understanding application vulnerabilities. For each of the 10 areas we will find a very detailed explanation of the vulnerability, how to detect it, how to prevent it, and a detailed example of how an attack on the issue might be carried out.

[1]https://www.owasp.org/index.php/Category:OWASP_Top_Ten_Project.

Software Development Life Cycle

The inclusion of security into the Software Development Life Cycle (SDLC) is a key area to include in training for developers. There are a nearly innumerable variety of approaches to this with one of the commonly used being the Microsoft Secure Development Lifecycle (SDL) [4]. The SDL process includes training, requirements, design, implementation, verification, release, and response, as shown in Fig. 8.1.

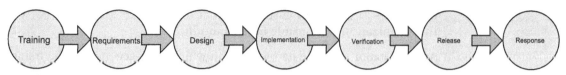

FIGURE 8.1
Microsoft secure development lifecycle process.

Although it is not particularly important that the SDL process specifically be the one to be followed, it is important there be some methods of ensuring that security is adequately represented in the SDLC.

Training for Management

In addition to the general areas that we discussed earlier managers need a leadership-appropriate version of the technical training that we discussed earlier and also need to know how to promote the security message. Additionally, they need to know what they are responsible and accountable for the security of.

Compliance

Managers need to understand the requirements that they and those that work for them have for compliance. In many cases, especially in technology management, there will be a variety of compliance requirements brought about by sensitive data that fall under their purview. PCI, PII (personally identifiable information), PHI (protected health information), HIPAA, NERC (North American Electric Reliability Corporation), and any number of other types of regulated data bring with them varied and sometimes conflict sets of rules and it is vital that managers have a sufficient understanding of the controls that govern these areas.

In addition to regulatory compliance, managers also need to understand what internal policies and procedures govern their daily activities. To provide guidance for the personnel, programs, and services for which they are responsible, we need to be sure that our managers are properly trained on what the particulars and expectations are and how to appropriately communicate the security message for these areas.

Sensitive and Regulated Data

In the area of sensitive and regulated data, in addition to the compliance requirements already discussed earlier in this chapter, managers need to understand specifically what information is sensitive and what rules govern the use of said data in any form in which they might appear.

Managers also need to know what their requirements are for loss of sensitive and regulated data, as it is all too common for such data to be accidentally divulged, lost, or otherwise inappropriately exposed. Additionally, they should know what, if any, their responsibilities are for reporting such data losses to victims or customers, or at least how to contact the party in the organization responsible for such notifications.

Another major area of data handling in which managers need to be trained is what the requirements are for disposal of sensitive or regulated data and what policies or procedures govern such activities. Inappropriate or insecure disposal of sensitive data could lead directly to a major breach.

Enforcing Security Policy

Managers should understand the requirements for enforcing security policy and secure practices for which they are responsible. Managers should be able to walk through an area and look for policy issues such as unsecured or improperly discarded sensitive data such as credentials written down and posted in working areas, printer matter of a sensitive nature left on printers, or other issues such as unlocked and unattended workstations or secured doors that have been propped open. They should also understand what the requirements are for reporting such issues when they are found.

We should also educate managers on the need to fairly and consistently enforce security policies. Security policies are in place to protect the organization and its customers and need to be followed uniformly. Inconsistent application of security policies can lead to a number of negative endings, including enabling attackers to successfully penetrate the security controls around our organization's environments.

Incident Response

Even, or perhaps especially, in the case where a manager is not part of a technology organization or of information security, he or she should have at least a high-level idea of what should and should not be done in the case of a security incident, whether the incident is internal or external in origin.

They should understand that data, hosts, and networks involved in a security incident need to be handled based on established processes so as not to, whether accidentally or purposefully, alter any evidence of what exactly took place. They should understand that tampering with any involved systems may render data that might later be used to investigate what exactly took place, or perhaps even legally prosecute those involved, unusable entirely. Particularly in the case of issues involving internal personnel, we should very carefully communicate what is expected of a manager in these types of situations.

TRAINING AND AWARENESS METHODS

There are a number of ways and means that we can use to communicate our training and awareness efforts to our user base. We can conduct training classes with a live instructor; employ computer-based training; provide various security-related media to users, play games, or run contests that have a security focus; give away items designed to bring security to mind, or any of a great number of other methods. The important part is not that we do any particular thing, but that we communicate effectively and are successful at modifying user behavior in a positive direction. Additionally, it must be done often; annual training is not effective in modifying behaviors. Ultimately, a successful program will more than likely end up employing a variety of methods.

Instructor-Led Training

Instructor-led training, as it sounds, is the traditional training scheme with a group of people listening to the instructor talk in real time. This could mean that a group of people gather in a single location or that the instructor is broadcast while speaking. This method is particularly useful where the people being trained are central to an office or location where new hire intake takes place.

One of the most important parts of this method is that it allows the instructor in interact with the audience in some fashion. This interaction enables the audience to ask questions of the instructor and the instructor to engage the audience by asking questions of them and by prompting them to relay their personal experiences with the subject matter being discussed at any given time. To allow this to happen, classes must be smaller (10–20 people).

Audience involvement is critical to ensuring that the subject matter is being grasped by the audience and provides some opportunity for in-flight modification of the content to suit a particular audience. Ultimately, this provides a better and more engaging experience for both the instructor and the audience and will result in an overall more successful training. Retention from these classes is always higher.

Although somewhat less desirable, instructor-led training can also be recorded for future playback by those who were not present for the training or who were unable to attend at the time of its delivery. Although this does not provide the valuable opportunity for audience feedback, it can still be of some value. In the case that recorded training is to be used as the primary method of delivery, it should be followed up with some other method of ensuring audience engagement, such as quiz or other test of knowledge. Otherwise all we are ensuring is the ability of our audience to tolerate background noise for a period of time (or fast forward through it).

Computer-Based Training

Computer-based training, often referred to as CBTs, can be a very handy method of delivering training to large or widely distributed groups of people where having them in a single location is not desirable or feasible. CBTs generally enable users to work on training at a time and place of their choosing, although often impose some deadline for the training to be accomplished.

CBTs can vary widely in quality. On the low end, they may be nothing more than a slide presentation that requires the user to click on each slide to move through it in a "death by PowerPoint fashion." Just as is the case when sitting through a meeting consisting of a slide deck being read by someone, this does not generally provide a strong method of communicating important concepts to users.

On the opposite end of the CBT quality spectrum, such training can incorporate multimedia, periodic activities designed to require input and activity from the user such as clicking and dragging matching items, small incremental knowledge checks, and so on. These require a much higher level of engagement from the user to proceed through the training and often culminate with an overall assessment of how well the user absorbed the concepts.

In addition to standard training of a presentation-oriented nature, some training providers even offer security-themed training games and activities. These can be of particular utility in environments that include a larger number of younger or technologically skilled users.

In general the computer training environment can provide us with the opportunity to step slightly outside of the bounds of the standard training paradigm. Novel activities such as games can provide us with an opportunity to reach users more effectively.

Games/Contests

Gamification is "the process of adding games or game like elements to something (as a task) so as to encourage participation" [5]. Elements of gamification that apply to security awareness and training might include items such as:

- narrative/story
- social aspects (networking, status, pressure)
- measurements of progress (points, levels, badges, scoreboards)
- clear goals
- challenges and challenges of increasing complexity
- collaborative problem solving
- time-dependent rewards
- competition
- collecting/trading

If we couch our training, awareness, and evaluation efforts in the form of a game, we are considerably more likely to find willing participants. Few people will willingly spend time in training that does not directly impact their present or desired set of responsibilities, but many will cheerfully while away the hours in playing a game.

One very easy to setup and conduct example that fits very nicely with the standard instructor-led security training class is the quiz show. We can quickly put

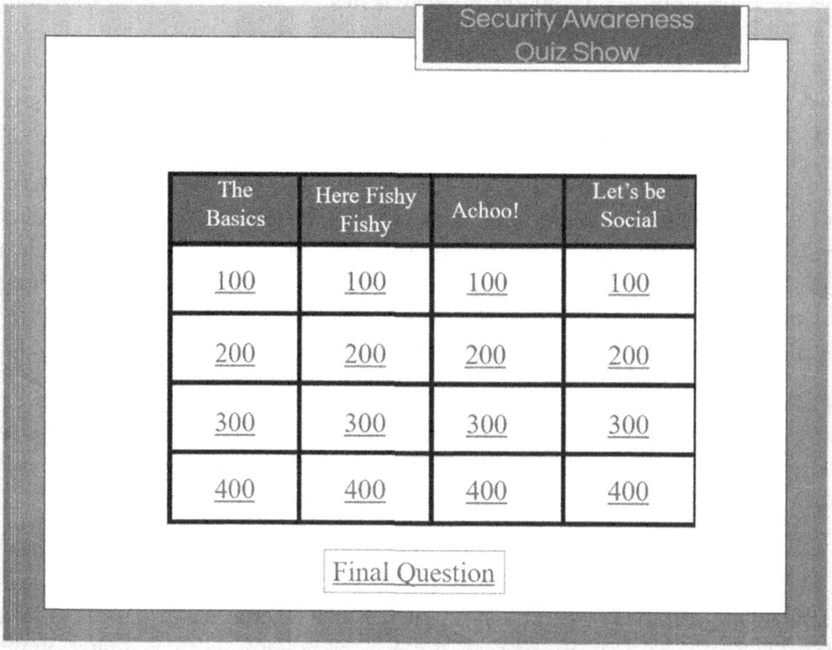

FIGURE 8.2
Security quiz show.

together a quiz show based on the common *Jeopardy* framework with categories based on our particular training efforts, such as that shown in Fig. 8.2.

This particular case touches on every one of the gamification elements that we mentioned earlier and lends quite a different atmosphere to what might otherwise be a relatively boring training class for those who do not have an inherent interest in information security. Ultimately, as with many of the other methods that we use for communicating security awareness topics, the more interesting and unusual methods will typically enjoy a much higher level of success. Novel methods will often stick with our trainees far better than the standard training "death by PowerPoint" tactics that seem to be all too unfortunately common in training classes the world over.

Security-Related Media

We can make use of a variety of security-related media items in support of our training and awareness efforts. This might include items such as:

- posters
- flyers
- newsletters

- security-branded notepads or sticky notes
- comics
- videos
- screensavers
- computer desktop backgrounds

Or any of a variety of other such vehicles. Although none of these items in isolation amounts to much, each of them draws attention to our program every time that someone sees, uses, or interacts with one of them. Media such as posters can easily be distributed to and displayed in a variety of areas, typically in gathering places such as break rooms, cafeterias, and other places where people will spend time sitting or standing in line.

Desk items such as sticky notes, screensavers, and desktop backgrounds can also be particularly effective, as these are often in close proximity to users for extended periods of time and will be noticed by them repeatedly, even if only for short periods of time as they move from one task to another.

A key item for any security-related media is that it will quickly age to the point of being unnoticed if it is not periodically refreshed. It is important to keep a relatively short cycle of updates to such items, where resources reasonably allow for this to happen. In the case of more costly items, such as higher-quality copies of printed posters, we can achieve this by rotating material from one location to another. In this way, at least the items in specific areas will change and be fresh to those who do not see all of the items across all locations. Novel or somewhat clever media items, such as the poster shown in Fig. 8.3 [6] will often draw more attention as well.

Giveaways

Giveaways are the standard items that we commonly see as conference Souvenirs, Wearables, and Gifts, i.e., t-shirts, pens, mugs, stress balls, small windup toys, and any of a number of other such items. Just as vendors at conferences give away branded examples of such items, we can use this same tactic to gain ongoing awareness of our security programs.

We can use giveaway items in a variety of ways. We can simply give them to people, such as those participating in information security training. If we send people away from our training with a security program branded pen or mug, we stand a slightly higher chance of having security pop into their mind whenever they use the item in question.

Perhaps more effectively, we can use giveaways as prizes for other security activities. If we can equate success or desirable actions with a physical prize, this can lend our item some level of status. This is a variety of gamification, as we discussed earlier in this chapter In this way, not only can we give away more

Some things
just shouldn't
be shared...

Keep Your Passwords to Yourself
Information Security Starts With You

Defend the Homeland. Defend the Information

FIGURE 8.3
Security awareness poster.

interesting items, as there will be presumably less of them than the security pen that we might give to everyone we train, but they can draw attention and awareness to the security program as well.

As we have said before in this chapter, every little bit helps when we are promoting security awareness. If we gain some level of increased security and positively modified behavior as a result of earmarking a tiny bit of our security budget for a few trinkets, then this is money well spent.

EVALUATE THE EFFECTIVENESS OF TRAINING

The real measure of training effectiveness comes when we evaluate explicit measures of our success. In many cases, this will mean developing metrics that we can use for such evaluation. We might, for example, count the number of incidents reported by users to determine whether we saw an increase or decline in incidents based on our training.

We may also choose to go with a more "rubber meets the road" type of evaluation and conduct activities like directly testing the responses of our users through activities, contests, or events or their reactions to realistic attack situations by including interacting with them in the scope of a penetration test.

Finally we need to conduct survey where our customers evaluate the security team for things like clear and understandable policies, useful training, and easy-to-follow processes. Open source tools like SurveyMonkey are useful for this.

Effectiveness Metrics

When we are developing metrics to measure our security awareness and training program, there are two major places that are useful for us to gather such data: the deployment of the program and the impact that the program is having as and after we have rolled it out. This does not preclude further metrics for measuring the progress of such a program, but these are common areas to measure when such programs are first being rolled out. More mature programs will likely see an ongoing change in metrics over time.

Metrics to measure deployment might include items such as [7]:

- Training completion—Number of users who have completed security awareness training.
- Communication methods—Types of training, who communication is directed to, and at what interval.
- Policy sign-off—Ensuring users have completed training, and signed an agreement of understanding of the policies.

Metrics to measure the impact of the program [7]:

- Phishing awareness—Number of people who failed during a phishing assessment.
- Phishing detection—Number of people who failed succeeded during a phishing assessment.
- Infected computers—Number of infected systems.
- Updated devices—Percentage of devices that are appropriately patched.
- Lost/stolen devices—Number of devices lost or stolen over a given period of time.
- Secure desktop—Number of users who lock their workstation while away from it.
- Passwords—Number of people using strong/complex passwords.
- Social engineering—Number of people who failed during a social engineering assessment.
- Sensitive data—Number of users posting sensitive company information on public facing media.

- Data wiping or destruction—Number of users properly following data destruction policies/processes.
- Facility physical security—Number of users who follow and enforce policies around physical access to facilities.

These metrics are, of course, simply a starting point on which to base a set measures that are appropriate for a specific organization. In any given environment the security focus will have particular emphases, i.e., credit cards, health care data, etc., and the security awareness metrics should be adjusted in accordance with these priorities. The key is to develop metrics that facilitate understanding and allow the capability owner to make an informed decision.

Counting Incidents

Counting incidents is one way that we can use to measure the effectiveness of our security awareness program. Logically, when we increase the level of training for how to respond to security incidents in our user population, and increase the level of awareness for such incidents existing in the first place, we would expect to see the number of reported security incidents go down, if not go down rather sharply. After all, our well-trained cadre of users should now be out making a more secure workplace as they carry out their appointed tasks, should they not? Unfortunately, or perhaps fortunately, no.

For example, what we can expect to see, when we have rolled out our awareness program in full force, is a sharp uptick in reported security incidents. Why would this be? For several reasons.

First, we have drawn awareness to security incidents existing. Although some subset of our users would have previously been both technically savvy enough and security aware enough to spot such incidents before our training, the general user population would not. We have given them a new set of tools and exhorted them to make use of them in the course of their daily activities. This means that we have now increased the likelihood that security issues will be detected and reported through the proper channels.

Second, we have greatly sensitized our users to the potential for security incidents to exist, whether they actually exist or not. For some period of time, we will likely see an uptick in jumping at shadows as relates to information security. We will get reports about every odd looking email, strange soliciting phone call, USB drive found in the hallway, and a wide variety of other such "incidents." This will calm down over time and as the idea of security awareness becomes less of a brand new thing.

Ultimately, we are likely to see sharp uptick in incidents, subsiding to a somewhat lesser level over time, but ultimately at a higher level than before we started the program. This is both a normal and a healthy expected result.

Testing Users

In this particular case, when we say testing this does not refer to penetration testing (we will come back to that momentarily). There are a variety of ways that we can test users before we proceed on to the rather heavy (and sometimes expensive) process of penetration testing.

When we are conducting training, and shortly after, we can literally test user behavior and knowledge. As we discussed earlier when discussing instructor-led training and CBTs, we can include quizzes and tests during and after training as a knowledge check. From a training perspective, this forces users to pay some level of attention when they would otherwise be staring out the window and wishing that they were somewhere else other than "wasting" a block of time in a training class. This gives us the opportunity to at least see if they were paying attention, although it may be somewhat boring.

As we discussed earlier in the section on gamification, we can also couch such testing in the form of a game. If we add elements of a game and of competition to our testing, we can sneak such evaluation on users while they are having fun. This also tends to give us a better result for purposes of evaluation, as we may have a larger share of the trainees' attention that we might have with a less enjoyable activity such as a quiz.

We can also conduct testing activities that edge more toward the direction of penetration testing without quite going all the way there. For example, we might try a very simple test of a particular item that we discussed in training. An easy case of this would be seeding a few USB drives around our facility with a "phone home" utility on them to see who picked them up and inserted them in a workstation. Numerous such tests could be conducted at a very small expense and a great return in terms of information about the secure or insecure behavior of our users. As we do this training it is important to decide if you are going to reward good behavior or openly punish poor performance and build the program to meet the style you feel is most effective.

Penetration Testing

Penetration testing is ultimately as close as we can get to a real world measure of the effectiveness of our training and awareness program. The ultimate goal of our program is to modify the behavior of our users in a more secure direction. When we conduct a penetration test, we can include in the scope items that test the reactions of our personnel in certain areas.

The most obvious of these categories is the broad category of social engineering attacks. Fortunately, such attacks are very easy to measure for success or failure; either the users fell prey to the attack or they did not. Some of the more obvious candidates for these types of attacks include standard social engineering efforts such as phishing email or phone calls, with the pretext and payload of such attacks being tuned to be feasible in the environment in which they are being conducted.

We can also intentionally include in our penetration testing items that should warn users of unusual activity taking place, such as unusual system loads or behaviors, attacks that we know will set off alert processes, attacks that are calculated to push users into areas where there are document process to be followed (such as requesting permission for a particular activity or process to be executed), and so on. If our users do not respond to the intentionally unusual activity in the proper fashion, or for that matter do not notice that it is taking place at all, then we know that we have further training to conduct and/or new areas in which we should focus our program to a greater extent.

Penetration testing, in particular the people-oriented portions, is a particularly important part of our security awareness and training program. In case after case where major breaches have happened, human failures to take appropriate actions have been at the heart of the failure to detect and block the inciting attack. Unfortunately, fixing such issues is not something that we can carry out with a simple technology purchase or configuration change. Fixing the insecure behaviors of people is a difficult prospect indeed. Ultimately penetrating testing will validate our incident response tools and training.

Report on Training Effectiveness

As with any other part of our security program, we will need to, at some point, report to our management on the effectiveness of our program. It is likely that the metrics that we discussed at the beginning of this section will feature heavily in such reporting. Although the full array of metrics may contain a greater level of detail than is useful or desirable for such reporting, they can certainly be used to inform in. Key performance indicators (KPIs) may be one useful way of rolling our metrics up into an easily reportable form to provide detail at a Goldilocks level (not too little, not too much, just right). KPIs are "quantifiable measurements, agreed to beforehand, that reflect the critical success factors of an organization" [8]. In the case of the metrics that we discussed earlier, we might have two KPIs to express the health of our security awareness program: one for the rollout of the program and another for the impact of the program.

The KPI for the rollout of the program, based on our metrics, would likely indicate the percentage of the user base that had been trained, with the ongoing state of the KPI being based on employee turnover versus training over time. In this fashion, we do not deliver the details of the individual metrics but can provide an overall view of the percentage of employees that are adequately trained at any given time.

Our KPI for impact, if we were trying to boil our collection of impact metrics up into a single item of performance data, would likely revolve around the metrics that indicate how our users performed when tested for appropriate response to a set of situations. In this case we might take the data from each individual metric that measured user behavior and take the average across all of them so that we could report a percentage of positive vs. negative responses.

Items such as these are often given just a few seconds of time in which to be reported during normal times and will generally need to be representable in graphical format on a presentation slide (think red, yellow, and green lights). In times of crises, however, such items are often given closer scrutiny, so backup slides containing the detailed data are always a useful thing to keep at the ready.

ACTIONS

Align awareness and training to stakeholders

- Work with the board, management, and individual contributors as stakeholders

Tune awareness and training for the audience

- Develop a program that covers the basic requirements for all users
- Develop supplementary material for technology users (IT and developers)
- Develop supplementary material for management

Develop metrics around the program to measure deployment

- Training completion
- Communication methods
- Policy sign-off

Develop metrics around the program to measure effectiveness

- Phishing awareness
- Phishing detection
- Infected computers
- Awareness survey
- Updated devices
- Lost/stolen devices
- Secure desktop
- Passwords
- Social engineering
- Sensitive data
- Data wiping or destruction
- Device physical security
- Facility physical security

References

[1] Palkon v. Holmes et al., No. 2:2014cv01234-Document 49 (D.N.J. 2014). In: Justia Law [Internet]. Available: http://law.justia.com/cases/federal/district-courts/new-jersey/njdce/2:2014cv01234/300630/49/.

[2] AfterDawn.com. Adobe kills off the "Flash" name to try to fix its reputation. In: AfterDawn [Internet]. Available: http://www.afterdawn.com/news/article.cfm/2015/12/03/adobe-kills-off-the-flash-name-to-try-to-fix-its-reputation.

[3] Types of security vulnerabilities [Internet]. Available: https://developer.apple.com/library/mac/documentation/Security/Conceptual/SecureCodingGuide/Articles/TypesSecVuln.html.

[4] Microsoft Security Development Lifecycle [Internet]. Available: https://www.microsoft.com/en-us/sdl/.

[5] Definition of GAMIFICATION [Internet]. Available: http://www.merriam-webster.com/dictionary/gamification.

[6] Kansas Adjutant General's Department – Command Information Products [Internet]. Available: http://kansastag.gov/NGUARD.asp?PageID=615.

[7] Information Security Awareness Training | Metrics Resources | SANS Securing The Human [Internet]. Available: http://securingthehuman.sans.org/resources/metrics.

[8] John Reh BF. What you need to know about key performance indicators. In: About.com Money [Internet]. Available: http://management.about.com/cs/generalmanagement/a/keyperfindic.htm.

CHAPTER 9

Security Compliance Management and Auditing

Information security compliance is both an operational and a legal concern for organizations in many industries today. However, it is not about the fear of lawsuits or fines (albeit this fear is well founded), but due to the increased reliance on information technology (IT), the value of information assets has increased significantly and maintaining repeatable, standardized operations relies on strong control compliance framework. Organizations depend mainly on IT to provide a platform for conducting business. As a result, controlling risks to information assets via security controls has become a dominating topic.

To comply with security practices, enterprises must develop comprehensive information security compliance management programs to comply with multiple regulations, such as Sarbanes–Oxley (SOX), Gramm–Leach–Bliley Act, Health Insurance Portability and Accountability Act (HIPAA), Payment Card Industry Data Security Standards (PCI DSS), and many others. These regulatory standards prescribe recommendations for protecting data and improving information security management in the enterprise.

- SOX requirements mean that any electronic communication must be backed up and secured with reasonable disaster recovery infrastructure,
- Health care providers that store or transmit e-health records, like personal health information, are subject to HIPAA requirements, and
- Financial services companies that transmit credit card data are subject to PCI DSS requirements.

157

Building a Practical Information Security Program. http://dx.doi.org/10.1016/B978-0-12-802042-5.00010-X

Failure to protect information assets may result in high financial and public cost and may also cause disruption of business activities, and even brand erosion. In some cases, such as with HIPAA, failure to achieve and maintain security compliance may potentially result in financial and legal penalties. What, precisely, is examined in a compliance audit will vary depending on whether an organization is a public or private company, what kind of data it handles, and if it transmits or stores sensitive financial data.

If managed properly, information security compliance standards can be used to strengthen an organization's overall information security program. Integrating compliance efforts with an organization's overall information security program can save money and time, reduce complexity, and help create long-term, sustainable solutions for an organization's information security challenges. In demonstrating security compliance, enterprises are better able to define and achieve specific IT security goals as well as mitigate the threat of network attacks through processes like vulnerability management.

ESTABLISHING AN INFORMATION SECURITY COMPLIANCE MANAGEMENT PROGRAM

An information security compliance management program comprises a minimum set of security requirements for protecting data that apply to any organization that stores, processes, or transmits that data. Maintaining information security compliance requires that an organization have well-defined programs, practices, and processes in place to review and reassess information security practices, even in highly dynamic business environments. To understand how an organization's security program performs on a day-to-day basis, organizations must implement an information security compliance program to continuously monitor and document the implementation, effectiveness, adequacy, and status of all of their security controls. These programs should be well aligned with the organization's business and security goals; address any changes within the organization, operating environment, and implemented technologies; and produce sufficient evidence to illustrate continued adherence to security requirements.

The information security leader should ensure the right stakeholders involved in the process—senior management support is essential for an information security compliance management program. Information security leader should use these various compliance mandates to get with senior leadership, who are often removed from day-to-day information security challenges and processes, to understand the compliance requirements and the organization's security state of compliance against these requirements.

Thankfully, senior leadership understands compliance; however, information security concepts, such as authentication, access controls, and logging and monitoring, continue to be abstract requirements to many senior executives. Senior leadership does understand many regulations come with penalties and fines that could impact the business, such as imprisonment for SOX noncompliance or fines for PCI DSS noncompliance. When discussing regular updates about compliance efforts and compliance projects, information security leader should also use the time to identify managers' security concerns and risk appetite, and educate senior leadership about information security efforts to reduce noncompliance risk.

For organizations that lack a senior executive dedicated to overseeing overall compliance, it is essential that a business risk steering committee be solicited to review the compliance audit process and outputs, including the recommendations. Be sure to include participants from all relevant business groups in the process, as well as line-of-business representatives. Even if the information security leader owns the information security compliance audit, great care should be taken to be sure the involvement of business risk steering committee usually comprises Internal Controls, Internal Audit, and Financial Executives, and the process is not dominated by the IT organization.

Once the information security leader has established support for a compliance management program with senior leadership, a qualified information security compliance manager should be assigned overall responsibility for these activities and be given adequate funding and the proper authority to effectively organize and allocate such resources. Maintaining security compliance requires a well-managed program to integrate security into the day-to-day activities of the organization. Ongoing compliance also requires centralized coordination of numerous resources, actions, projects, and people.

The information security compliance manager would be responsible for engaging management support, coordinating monitoring and assessment activities, and engaging key personnel or functional groups as part of the efforts to ensure all security functions, such as patching systems, security-log reviews, wireless network scans, internal/external vulnerability scans, and internal/external penetration tests are performed as required. Additionally, the information security compliance manager should be responsible for collecting, collating, and storing evidence to demonstrate security controls are operating effectively on a continuous basis. Although the compliance manager is not typically tasked with generating or organizing all of the evidence, the compliance manager would be responsible for making certain the evidence is prepared, indexed, and stored in a central repository for use during assessments or internal reviews. Often the compliance manager and team rely on governance, risk, and compliance (GRC) tools to manage the process through workflow and hold evidence for inspection.

PUBLISHING AN INFORMATION SECURITY COMPLIANCE POLICY

To ensure organizational understanding of the information security compliance management mandate, a policy is an important tool to state the mandate's objective, goals, purpose, roles, and responsibilities, and its relationship to the overall information security program. The policy formally articulates the requirements that assist management in defining a framework that ensures compliance with the overall information security goals with security-related laws, regulations, policies, standards, and contractual provisions to which their IT resources and data are subject. The policy also has ties to the subordinate procedures and guidelines that may explain the "how" compliance is implemented.

It is equally important to review and update the information security compliance management policy and procedures. As discussed in Chapter 4, the organization may have irrelevant or stale policies, lacks policies that are routinely adhered to, or does not follow the ones it does have in place. In any organization that relies on IT, policies need to be fluid and dynamic, and continually evaluated and updated for appropriateness toward changing IT environment or business conditions. The IT and information security functions should determine together which compliance policies need to be updated, which need to be overhauled, which need to be added, and which need to be retired.

DEPLOY AN INFORMATION SECURITY COMPLIANCE PROCESS

Organizations confronted with multiple regulatory requirements, as well as their own security policies, are often stretched about how to meet so many laws and regulations obligations. Some organizations allow information security compliance to be addressed by more than just the information security function. For example, they may allow the business units most directly affected by the regulatory requirement to perform their own compliance assessment in addition to the organizational compliance assessment and perhaps even a third Internal Audit assessment. As a result, efforts are often incomplete, redundant, duplicative, and even costly. In addition, these organizations may not have the rigor or discipline to execute an evidence-based audit and may simply "self-attest" to a state that is not reflected by reality.

A piecemeal approach may also undermine the integration of information security compliance into other institutional compliance programs, such as information privacy and institutional governance. For example, a decentralized approach to information security compliance management could make it harder to monitor and report the controls that are increasingly a part of audits. For all of these reasons, organizations should consider a unified approach to meeting information security compliance. By using a unified approach to information security compliance, organizations subject to multiple information security laws, regulations, and guidelines will be able to comply with all of them at one time. This is commonly known as a "test once, comply many" approach. By determining which organizational policies, laws, and regulations are applicable, the compliance team then conducts a comprehensive compliance analysis that covers these multiple requirements, and then recommends the minimum level of required safeguards to meet these requirements. Where there are conflicting requirements, such as password strength, encryption strength, or audit settings, compliance should focus on the most stringent requirement as a "high water mark."

Step 1: Determine Applicable Security Policies, Laws, and Regulations

The first step in the process is to determine the security policies, laws, and regulations applicable to the organization. This is an important preliminary step to set compliance's scope. This determination not only will assist in preparing the compliance assessment plan but also will guide the compliance assessor in selecting the information to be collected and the type of compliance assessment methodology that should be performed.

Identifying the appropriate requirements is not always a straightforward process. Depending on their activities and operations, organizations can be affected by a number of laws and regulations. In addition, some policies, laws, and regulations apply only to specific organizational departments or functional activities. In other cases, more than one requirement on the same control area or domain may be applicable. Once the applicable information security requirement law is determined, an appropriate information security risk or compliance analysis framework, such as International Organization for Standardization (ISO) 27004 or National Institute of Standards and Technology (NIST) 800-series, can be selected. It is often worth the effort to map these several requirements when the target of evaluation is governed by several information security framework requirements. For example, if the information system password authentication requirement for system access is six characters for one requirement, eight character for another, and eight characters and special characters for yet a third, it may be helpful for a single requirement (the most stringent) and evaluate the system accordingly.

The analysis model to be used will depend on the organizational type, applicable information security requirements, and information security framework aligned to both type and requirements. An example is a government agency that is aligned to NIST 800-series may require the compliance framework of NIST Special Publication 800-37 "Guide for Applying the Risk Management Framework to Federal Information Systems." A second example is a commercial entity that is aligned to ISO 27000-series may find the ISO 27004 method of risk management more appropriate. Some helpful qualifying questions can be asked to determine the scope and focus of the compliance assessment:

- What is the type of organization (i.e., privately held, publically traded, government agency)?
- What type of industry or markets does the business participate in?
- What type of information is stored, processed, transmitted?
- What processes have legal or regulatory implications (i.e., does the organization provide health care service, process credit cards for payment purposes)?

Step 2: Prepare the Information Security Compliance Management Plan

After the information security compliance requirements are identified, a thorough compliance management plan is prepared by the compliance manager. This management plan is used to guide the individual compliance activities— number and type of compliance audits by business unit or entity, schedules of the compliance activities including senior leadership reviews, policy and supporting procedure and guideline updates, staffing mixes and training requirements for the conduct of audits, and any technology road maps for tools used during compliance audits. This is traditionally an annual process, adjusted periodically as schedules or resources become released or constrained.

Step 3: Data Collection and Asset Identification

Information gathering includes the identification of assets to be protected, document review, and interviews with both management and other stakeholders. The individuals who are interviewed may be line-of-business personnel, functional staff, senior management, legal counsel, audit and compliance personnel, and, of course, the IT staff. It may also involve vendors and other third parties, particularly if certain functions are outsourced but are in scope of the audit. The scope of the interviews will differ slightly, depending on the state, federal, and international laws and regulations that are applicable.

The data collection process will review information security technical, operational, and risk management practices, processes, and procedures. Technical security reviews includes asset management, configuration management, security management, as well as assessment of IT architecture, application, and network policies. Operational security includes vulnerability management, patch management, incident management, business continuity/disaster recovery, and other operational service or functions. Risk management reviews cover policies and procedures, risk assessments, compliance audits, third-party security reviews, and other analytical functions in managing and governing IT security risk. It is also important to ensure that physical security is included to evaluate compliance for the protection of information security facilities.

Evidence is collected through either manual or automated methods, mainly documentary, interviews, and automated collection through system or security tools. Documentary evidence include written policies and procedures, Internet policies and procedures, sanctions and disciplinary procedures, and other documents evidencing organizational efforts to protect information, such as contracts, procedures for assigning, modifying, or removing access rights, and password-management policies. Auditors will generally ask chief information officers, chief technology officers, and IT administrators a series of pointed questions over the course of an audit. Interviews are particularly helpful to elicit how the program is implemented and personal observations of its effectiveness. Some important areas to cover during interviews are:

- the individual(s) responsible for information privacy and security (organizational and departmental levels);
- information assets that need to be protected to support the business and operations;
- how the information security program is structured; how compliance policies and procedures are implemented and integrated with other activities;
- how well departments work together to ensure that information security practices are uniform; which third parties have access to the institution's information system.

IT administrators prepare for compliance audits using event log managers and robust change management software to allow tracking and documentation authentication and controls in IT systems. These tools' output may include what users were added and when, who has left the company, whether user IDs were revoked and which IT administrators have access to critical systems. Beyond the common system management tools, the growing technological landscape of GRC software now enables the IT staff to quickly show auditors that the organization is in compliance.

Step 4: Perform Risk Analysis

In Step 4, the collected data are integrated into the selected risk analysis (e.g., organizational, ISO, or NIST frameworks). The quality and effectiveness of compliance risk analysis results will depend heavily on how much data were collected in Step 3. The compliance risk analysis includes technical, operational, and management security including organizational context and considerations.

Step 5: Report Findings and Recommendations

The results of the compliance risk analysis are then documented in an information security compliance audit report. The information security compliance audit report should list organizational context, identified threats and vulnerabilities, current controls, and control effectiveness or even absence. To ensure relevancy and due diligence, the information security compliance audit report should reference specific sections or paragraphs of the applicable security regulations for both existing and missing controls. The plan should encompass all the safeguards identified in the risk analysis and also include procedures for the selection of security system vendors or service providers, and the installation of security systems or services. To maximize the report's effectiveness, the information security compliance audit report should also contain an action plan and milestone schedule for implementing the necessary changes to attain compliance with applicable laws and regulations.

Step 6: Execute the Implementation Plan

The implementation plan provided in the information security compliance audit report is executed in this step. At this stage of the compliance process, it is important to integrate all new controls for meeting information security compliance with other compliance efforts currently under way (e.g., financial, contracts, legal). The integration of compliance programs will ensure uniformity and consistency across the compliance activities, or at the very least avoid duplication of effort redundancy. For example, rationalization and harmonization of compliance activities to support information security regulations can potentially save time, money, and other resources and procedures.

Step 7: Periodically Monitor, Test, Review, and Modify the Information Security Compliance Management Program

Information security, as any IT activity, is an ongoing process. Maintaining a state of continuous compliance requires focused effort and coordination. Due to the changing technology landscape, information security functions should continuously monitor and test the effectiveness of implemented controls against known or potential threats. This involves testing applications and networks or applications against emerging threats and recommending actions when threats are present and vulnerabilities are discovered. Organizations that are accustomed to traditional approaches of information security compliance that focus primarily on annual audits may find it difficult to build in the people, processes, and technology necessary to support sustained compliance. Organizations should perform periodic compliance risk analysis to validate that control selection and implementation features continue to be reasonable, appropriate, and effective.

INFORMATION SECURITY COMPLIANCE MANAGEMENT IN MERGERS AND ACQUISITIONS

Mergers and acquisitions (M&A) can be extremely effective mechanisms for companies to achieve important business objectives. Information security and privacy compliance requirements play a critical role because they may impact the acquirer's business objectives, regulatory profile, and valuation model, particularly if the new acquisition introduces increased risk of an information security or privacy-related liability. Whether the M&A goal is gaining access to a new market, acquiring new technology, or gaining economies of scale, the acquiring organization needs to develop an information security compliance approach that addresses information security and privacy concerns that may manifest themselves before, during, and after the M&A. As the information security team reviews acquisition targets, as well as the M&A team's approach to evaluating targets, the team should consider the following elements:

- If the acquisition goal is expansion into new industries or geographic regions, there may be new regional regulatory or legal requirements for information security and privacy. It is important to identify what new markets will be entered. If the acquisition involves expansion into highly regulated sectors (e.g., health care, financial, business targeting children as consumers, etc.), then the information security program may require a change in the face of changing compliance obligations, both domestic and international, for the organization.
- If new business processes are introduced with new data types or categories transmitted, processed, or stored between the two parties, this may introduce a different level of required security or privacy compliance. During the due diligence process, if the acquirer finds that the acquisition target involves cross-border data transfers or privacy regulations, the acquirer will need to explore the target's compliance for transmission security. For example, if the seller or target has certified to the EU–US Safe Harbor replacement program ("Privacy Shield"), the acquirer will want to review any previous Safe Harbor assessments, as well as its publicly available Safe Harbor certification. If the seller or target is subject to HIPAA, the buyer would want to evaluate its HIPAA compliance measures. The compliance risk profile of the buyer or seller might change post sale.
- If the motivation for acquisition is the introduction of a new product, service, or technology, then the types of data categories or sensitivity of

privacy information must be identified. What privacy policies, notices, and other compliance efforts will be required to support new products, services, or technologies? This becomes particularly relevant if the acquisition uses the acquired technology in a different manner than earlier designed. For example, using a new platform for processing data types for which it was not designed may require rework and additional cost to the acquirer, and therefore may dilute the value proposition of the acquisition by introducing more cost to the transaction.

Another information security compliance concern is the M&A process itself. Both parties should be sensitive that sometimes providing other parties (such as the acquirer in an M&A) with the personal information of employees or clients can itself be a breach of privacy policies or laws. Questions should be asked before the diligence process actually takes place to ensure no violations will occur with performing the diligence process. Likewise, another aspect of due diligence is third-party information security compliance. It is during the diligence process that large amounts of sensitive and confidential information will be shared with bankers, attorneys, consultants, third-party vendors, and other parties. No matter how secure an organization is and how many process steps are taken to secure their data, both parties are reliant on third parties that host, access, and store the target organization's data. Parties, particularly the target company, should carefully assess third-party compliance to information security practices that will be hosting their data during the diligence process, particularly in their online data rooms.

SUMMARY

The increased number of government-mandated and private contractual information security requirements has caused organizations to view information security as another aspect of regulatory or contractual compliance. The existence of fines, penalties, or loss (including brand erosion) has also increased the appetite to implement comprehensive information security practices, such as information security compliance management. This approach begins by reviewing all of the information security requirements imposed by the emerging statutory, regulatory, and contractual legal standards. These standards are then compared with the more established information security standards. After a thorough risk assessment and analysis, the legal standards and the information security standards are blended to create a complete information security compliance program. A unified approach to information security compliance thus enables organizations not only to address identified risks but also to comply with the law.

ACTIONS

Identify the business need for an information security compliance program; compliance programs do not exist unto themselves.

- Industry involvement, regional orientation, business processes or product/services, and information types will generally indicate a requirement to protect. The compliance program will tie the requirement and validation together as a business requirement.

Develop an information security compliance management policy and supporting documentation according to the compliance requirement (legal, regulatory).

- An overarching policy provides the basis and justification of the information security compliance program. Subordinate procedures, guidelines, and checklists then provide the "tools" for implementing the program. Periodic information security compliance policy and other documentation reviews should be conducted as regulations and standards change—the policy, as a minimum, should be reviewed annually for relevancy and effectiveness.

Identify stakeholders that will champion the information security compliance management program.

- Usually these stakeholders will be involved in other compliance or compliance-related activities; the chief financial officer and chief compliance officer are typically the best champions for a compliance-based program that reduces financial risk, as well as any other compliance risks to the business that may cause some degree of materiality to the business.

Design and develop a compliance management process that is easy to understand and follow.

- Ensure traceability to the legal requirements to compliance audit framework—the requirement must have direct correlation to the audited control and data that support the analysis. Failure to demonstrate traceability will cause some to call into question the reason for the compliance audit if it is not relevant. Simplicity in compliance audit execution will be much more palatable than onerous, time-consuming audit processes.

Deliver business value through clear and concise reporting of findings and recommendations.

- Ensure that these recommendations are vetted against other risk and compliance management recommendations to eliminate redundancy and duplication. The overall finding should be easy to understand in business terms and relevant to the business risk than simply technical risk. The business leader who cannot translate the compliance gap to the effect on the business is less apt to invest in gap remediation than one who easily understands the gap and necessity to close it due to business impact.

Ensure information security has a role in M&A.

- M&A can have an impact on the organizational compliance posture through the integration of new business processes and information categories between the acquirer and target organizations. During due diligence, the information security team should understand the target acquisition compliance requirement, how the target is meeting them, and if any liability or risk of failures may be introduced into the acquirer's portfolio of information security risks. Post acquisition, the information security program will need to integrate the new acquisition into the existing information security compliance program.

CHAPTER 10

Information Security Program Metrics

Information security metrics can help organizations verify that their security controls are in compliance with a policy, process, or procedure; identify their security strengths and weaknesses; and identify security trends, both within and outside the organization's control. Studying trends allows an organization to monitor its security performance over time and to identify changes that necessitate adjustments in the organization's security posture. At a higher level, these benefits can be combined to help an organization achieve its mission by evaluating its compliance with legislation and regulations; improving the performance of its implemented security control; and answering high-level business questions regarding security, which facilitate strategic decision making by the organization's highest levels of management.

An information security metric quantifies the component activities of a process, person, or product via a predefined system of measurement. Information security metrics are simple calculations or formulas that seek to measure and manage information security processes like risk management, compliance management, application security, and cybersecurity, to name a few. Information security metrics describe:

- what exactly is being measured,
- specific units of measurement (e.g., percentages, ratios, indexes, numbers),
- how it is to be measured, and
- which data source will be used to collect the measurements.

The term metric is often used to refer to the measurement of performance, but it is clearer to define metrics and measures separately. A metric is an abstract,

Building a Practical Information Security Program. http://dx.doi.org/10.1016/B978-0-12-802042-5.00011-1

somewhat subjective attribute, such as how well an information security program secures the organization against external threats or how effective is the organization's incident response team. A measure is a concrete, objective attribute, such as the percentage of systems within an organization that are fully patched, the length of time between the release of a patch and its installation on a system, or the level of access to a system that a vulnerability in the system could provide. A table of definitions and sources of the definitions is provided.

Definition	Source
Metrics—data used to facilitate decision making and improve performance and accountability through collection, analysis, and reporting of relevant performance-related data	NIST SP 800-55 Rev. 1, performance measurement guide for information security
Measure—a variable to which a value is assigned as the result of measurement. Often synonymous with metric.	ISO/IEC 27004, information technology—IT security techniques—information security management—measurement
Measurement—the process of obtaining information about the effectiveness of information security management systems and controls using a measurement method, a measurement function, an analytical model, and decision criteria	ISO/IEC 27004, information technology—IT security techniques—information security management—measurement

ISO/IEC, *International Organization for Standardization/International Electrotechnical Commission;* NIST, *National Institute of Standards and Technology.*

Many information security metrics programs have focused on collecting individual measures with little thought on how the measures could be combined or transformed into metrics. A more optimal approach is to first select the information security metric, and then determine what measures they can perform that produce the metrics. By collecting and analyzing groups of measures, the information security analyst can approximate the metric.

An organization should also have multiple levels of metrics, each geared toward a particular type of audience. The audience of information security metrics includes senior executives, lines-of-business management, and functional support staff including the information technology (IT) and information security staff: strategic decision making, business risk management, and operational performance monitoring benefit from an information security metrics program.

- Strategic decision making support. Security metrics information aid different kinds of strategic decision making (e.g., industry or market entry, program planning, resource allocation, product and service selection). Information security metrics and benchmarking can introduce critical information on the organization's competitiveness in the market relative to its security, perceived or not.

- Risk management. An organization that understands its security posture, likely understands its level of security risk relative to its IT management control systems. Risk management metrics assist the business, at multiple levels, to understand what information assets need protection, what are threats to the assets, management controls effectiveness, what gaps exist, and new controls need to be added.
- Operational information security monitoring and reporting. Monitoring the operational IT environment and its security posture can determine compliance with the security requirements (e.g., policy, procedures, and regulations), as well as gauge the performance of specific operational security programs and technical controls, effectiveness of security controls under stresses, provide a basis for trend analysis, and identify specific for improvement.

For example, information security management might be interested in higher-level metrics regarding the organization's security posture, such as the overall effectiveness of the organization's incident response handling capabilities. Technical information security staff might be interested in lower-level metrics related to the effectiveness of particular types of security controls, such as intrusion detection rates or user access violations. Lower-level information security metrics facilitate making more tactical decisions, whereas higher-level information security metrics are well suited for making more strategic decisions. The lower-level metrics are often used as input to the higher-level metrics.

Information security metrics and measurements can be used to facilitate decision making and improve performance and accountability through the collection, analysis, and reporting of relevant performance-related data. Information security metrics must be based on information security performance goals and objectives. Likewise, organizations can also use information security metrics and measures to set targets as goals, and determine success or failure against the targets. For example, if an organization determines that 70% of its information systems is compliant with an antivirus policy. The organization could set a target threshold of 90%, implement changes in its processes or procedures to increase compliance, and then measure compliance quarterly to determine if the target has been achieved. Targets are generally very organizationally specific and are based on operational baselines in the environment.

BUILDING THE SECURITY METRICS PROGRAM

To facilitate understanding and acceptance at all levels of a new security metrics program, it is advisable to ground the program in a well-defined process in the development and sustainment of the initiative. The eight steps below could be used to guide the process of establishing a security metrics program.

Step 1. Identify the Stakeholders

Executive buy-in is the key to successfully deploying an information security metrics program. As highlighted earlier, in the case of initiatives that have a perceived lack of benefits or could affect unwanted cultural change, it is inevitable that many who will be affected by a metrics implementation effort will question it. Some may even work against it. For that reason, it is critical that a high-level executive sponsor visibly supports the metrics program.

Once the sponsor is identified, stakeholders are likewise identified (usually with the help of the sponsor). Stakeholder generally corresponds to the scope of the information security program. Senior executives who have interest in the strategic decision-making benefits of the metrics program will typically be the chief information officer, chief financial officer, chief privacy officer, and chief human relations officer and general counsel. Those who have business risk management concerns generally consist of the lines-of-business and functional support leaders. Operational metrics will involve both functional and operational staff responsible for execution of their management scope.

Step 2: Define Metrics Program Goals and Objectives

Information security metrics program development and maintenance take considerable effort and divert resources; it is critical that the goal(s) and objectives of the program be well defined and agreed upon. For the metrics program to demonstrate value and effectiveness, it is very important to tie metrics to business goals. Statements of objectives should also indicate high-level actions that must be collectively accomplished to meet the goal(s). Such goals may include:

- cost avoidance from security incidents
- higher information security performance
- lower operational risks and errors
- greater regulatory compliance
- meeting cost and schedule targets for information security projects
- return on investment for key information security projects
- end-user productivity

Step 3: Decide Which Metrics to Report

Any underlying corporate framework could dictate what metrics are needed. This step would be to identify those specific security processes. A compliance-based approach would assess how closely established security standards are being followed. There are several standards-based information security metrics frameworks that have been formalized to assess an overall organizational information security program. Many stem from regulatory or legal requirements, such as Sarbanes–Oxley, Health Insurance Portability and Accountability Act, or European Network and Information Security Agency.

Others are related to industry-based compliance framework (e.g., Payment Card Industry Data Security Standard). Although some organizations may choose to design, implement, and deploy their own security measures, the adoption of standards and guidelines for security measurement greatly improves the quality of an organization's measurement program, and allows organizations to better communicate their security postures with others that share the same framework, and allow benchmarking with other external organizations. Another benefit is if the organization adopts a policy framework based on standards, then the complementary metrics framework is readymade to adopt and tailor for conformance. Two such frameworks, ISO 27004:2009 Information Security Management Measurement and National Institute of Standards and Technology (NIST) Special Publication 800-55 Revision 1 Performance Measurement Guide, deserve special mention.

ISO 27004:2009—Information Security Management—Measurement

In the ISO/IEC 27000 series, information security metrics now has its own ISO standard, ISO/IEC 27004:2009, and has been integrated into the revised information security management standard ISO 27001:2013. ISO recognition has led to a significant rise in the use of information security metrics and potential value to the information security posture of the organization. ISO/IEC 27004; 2009 concerns measurements relating to information security management. The standard is intended to help organizations measure, report on, and hence systematically improve the effectiveness of their information security management systems.

It provides guidance on the development and use of measures and measurement to assess the effectiveness of an implemented information security management system and controls or groups of controls, as specified in ISO/IEC 27001:2013. This would include policy, information security risk management, control objectives, controls, processes, and procedures, and support the process of its revision, helping to determine whether any of the processes or controls need to be changed or improved. ISO 27004:2009 articulates core information security metrics that will be required to demonstrate conformance to the standard. If core metrics were to be clearly defined, companies could collect industry-wide statistics, and use them to benchmark performance and progress. In addition, the ISO standard does allow for the creation of customized metrics and measurements. The measurement process used in ISO/IEC 27004 consists of the steps of:

- developing measures,
- operating measurement program,
- analyzing and reporting results, and
- evaluating and improving the measurement program itself.

The measurement model in ISO/IEC 27004:2009 provides a detailed top-down and bottom-up structure for identifying the information that is being sought from the measures, the individual attributes required to construct individual measures, and a hierarchical structure for rolling up and consolidating the data with increasing complexity.

NIST Special Publication 800-55 Revision 1—Performance Measurement Guide

The NIST in the United States has also made significant contributions to the production of guidelines and definitions on the use of security metrics. NIST Special Publication 800-55 Revision 1, Performance Measurement Guide for Information Security, describes the processes and methodologies that link information system level security performance to organizational agency performance through the organization's strategic planning processes. By doing so, the processes and methodologies help demonstrate how information security contributes to accomplishing organizational strategic goals and objectives. NIST cites that the performance measures developed according to NIST SP 800-55 will enhance the ability of organizations to respond to government mandates and initiatives (i.e., Federal Information Systems Management Act or FISMA). The measurements standard focuses on three key measurement categories: implementation measures, effectiveness/efficiency measures, and impact measures. NIST SP 800-55 recommends when establishing a measurements program, the organization should follow the steps of:

- mapping measures of the information security program performance to information security goals and objectives across the range of security controls;
- mapping measures corresponding to security control families or individual security controls directly to the individual security control(s);
- use the data describing the security control's implementation and security program performance to generate required measures.

In the absence of any preexisting framework, a top-down or a bottom-up approach for determining which metrics might be desirable could be used. Meaningful and well-designed metrics and measurements for a business or organization are created and selected by carefully defining their scope and purpose. In this form, metrics can be used to address a wide range of information security management issues including measurement of progress in achieving goals and objectives, adherence to internal control procedures, justification of budgets and investment, and effectiveness of training and awareness program.

The selection of the metric should be able to answer what objective is being sought. Ouedraogo, et al. (2013) [1], assert that a good metric should always satisfy the criteria of meaningfulness, measurability, correctness, and usability. *Meaningfulness* requires that the metrics and measurements should be focused and their value should be easily recognizable and apparent to the intended audience. *Correctness* is the metric's context, completeness, and objectivity to what is being measured. *Measurability* requires the metric to have the attainability or availability with sufficient accuracy to be measured. The criteria of *usefulness* entail the metric's efficiency, scalability, and cost-effectiveness. Each metric should be questioned for its appropriateness using a standard set of questions.

Questions Relevant to Meaningfulness
- Is the metric meaningful in the context of its use?
- Is the metric meaningful to the measurer in the context of its use?
- Is the metric meaningful to the audience in the context of its use?
- Are the metric and associated measurements clearly formulized?
- Are only important parameters considered in the metric?
- Is the metric applicable to the planned decision making?
- Does the metric support comparability?
- Are the metrics and related measurements useful in the decision making?

Questions Relevant to Measurability
- Can the measurement data be provided from the scope of the assessment?
- Are the measurement data available?
- Are the same results returned if a measurement is reproduced in the same context, with exactly the same conditions?
- Are the same results returned if a measurement is repeated in the same context, with exactly the same conditions?
- Are the same results returned if a measurement is reproduced in the same context, with exactly the same conditions by different measurers?

Questions Relevant to Correctness
- Does the metric and what is being measured correlate?
- Are the results of the metric consistent enough?
- Are the results of the metric able to accurately depict the attributes of the measured element?
- Is the metric able to predict the security risk for the purposes of metric?
- Are we measuring the attribute that we really want to measure?
- Do we know enough about an attribute before it is reasonable to consider measuring it?
- Do we know enough about the context before it is reasonable to consider measuring it?

- Does the collection of measurements cover the objectives to a sufficient degree?
- Can the measurement results be biased by the measurer's beliefs or actual feeling?

Questions Relevant to Usefulness

- Are the measurement results kept within the defined limits or the measurement window?
- Are adequate measurements achieved while only consuming the minimum amount of undesired resources?
- Are adequate measurements achieved while only consuming minimal costs?
- Are adequate measurements achieved while only consuming the minimum amount of effort and time?

A second good metrics selection framework that helps indicate which security goals are being met and drives actions to improve the security posture of the organization is that which is *SMART* (specific, measurable, attainable, repeatable, and time dependent). Whatever framework is used to develop and select the appropriate metrics, it should be easily understood and mutually agreed to by those who are using and reviewing the measurements.

Step 4: Establish Targets and Threshold

In this step appropriate targets are identified and thresholds set. To increase or maintain an acceptable level of information security, organizations must set targets and performance thresholds at which corrective action must be taken. A target is the desired level of performance, as indicated by measures that represent success at achieving a defined outcome. A threshold is a level, rate, or amount at which something comes into effect; in this case, a threshold is where the measurement crosses from acceptable to unacceptable state. See Appendix A for thresholds as depicted by an information security scorecard.

One method in establishing targets and thresholds is using historical measures. It can be helpful to use measures that the information security organization has already gathered to establish a baseline, or starting point, for a target. If historical data are unavailable, consider using information from outside data sources to benchmark, or compare, your performance data with those of other comparable organizations. The information security leader not only should review industry-specific data resources for possible targets and best practices, but also may find national and global metrics provided by SANS Institute, NIST, and other publications helpful. Technical benchmarking is also a manner of comparing the organization's performance and practices against peer groups within the industry or noted "best practice" organizations outside the industry. These technical benchmarks can be found in various industry associations or professional research organizations, such as the Corporate Executive Board, Gartner, and others. Then set targets that seem reasonable in light of the benchmarking information.

Step 5: Develop Strategies for Collecting Metrics Data

Once an organization has identified its metrics, it then needs to determine what measures can feasibly be collected to support those metrics. These strategies should specify the source of the data, the frequency of data collection, and who is responsible for raw data accuracy, data compilation into measurements, and generation of the metric. Organizations should seek opportunities to use existing data sources and automated collection mechanisms because of the cost of implementing and maintaining new systems and software simply for data collection purposes. As measures are collected, organizations need a way to analyze them and generate reports for the metrics they support. Organizations can analyze the measures and metrics in many ways, such as grouping them by business group, market industry, geographic location, logical division within the organization, information system type, and/or information system criticality.

Organizations should also favor measures that can be collected via automated means because they are more likely to be more accurate than manual collection and can also be collected at any time. These sources of data can be system configuration files, system logs, firewall logs, audit reports, and user surveys. Although most of these sources of data were distributed across the enterprise, and there were few automated tools available, new products such as governance, risk, and compliance (GRC) applications have been introduced into the marketplace to make data collection, analysis, and reporting much more cost-effective. These GRC applications roll up measures into metrics and present the metrics in a security dashboard format, with the measures underlying each metric available through drill-down. This allows a dashboard user to see the values of the presented metrics and changes in those metrics over time, as well as to examine the metrics and measures comprising those metrics.

Step 6: Determine How Metrics Will Be Reported

No information security metrics program effort is effective if the results are not communicated well. Executives may be accustomed to dealing with financial and other trend lines, but since information security is not a core competency for management, complex information security–related data should be presented in a concise, well-understood format. The context, format, frequency, distribution method, and responsibility for reporting metrics should be defined up front, so that the end product can be visualized early on by those who will be involved in producing the metrics and those who will be using them for decision making. Graphic representations are particularly effective.

Another aspect is the distribution or presentation of the information security metrics to targeted audiences. Revisiting the list of stakeholders will help organize the right topics with the right audiences. Senior executives who have interest in the strategic decision-making metrics will typically be the chief information officer, chief financial officer, chief people officer, chief human resources officer, and general counsel. Lines-of-business and functional support leaders will have an interest in the business risk management-related metrics. Operational metrics will be interesting to functional and operational staff responsible for execution of their management scope. Some information security metrics may be meaningful only to the information security manager and staff, and should not be distributed further. However, some tactical information security metrics are required to help articulate remedial actions with the organization, particularly when funding is concerned.

Step 7: Create a Remediation Action Plan

Where the information security metrics reveal gaps, particularly critical gaps, a remediation action plan should accompany the report. A remediation action plan should contain all tasks that need to be accomplished to address the gap along with the gap owner, expected completion dates, and deliverables. As mentioned in Step 2, action items should be directly traceable to the goals and objectives. Highlighting the traceability of actions in the plan to goals and objectives is useful why a given action is important. Another best practice in action planning is the incorporation of a verification or testing process to ensure the desired outcome has been realized. Lastly, an accountable executive or manager, usually the gap owner, should be required to inspect and validate the action closure.

Step 8: Conduct a Formal Program Review Cycle

An information security metrics program will require a formal, regular review of the metrics and measurements at least on an annual basis. Metrics that become stale or irrelevant are an indicator for a program refresh. Some guiding questions should be used to test for program effectiveness:

- Are the metrics useful in determining new courses of action for the overall security program?
- How much effort is it taking to generate the metrics?
- Is the value derived worth that effort?

These and other similar questions will be important to answer during the annual review process. A complementary approach is benchmarking within and outside the organization and industry to help identify new developments and opportunities to fine-tune the program.

INFORMATION SECURITY METRICS AND KEY PERFORMANCE INDICATORS

A key performance indicator (KPI) is a metric used to evaluate factors that are crucial to the success of an organization. KPIs are quantifiable measurements, agreed to beforehand, that reflect the critical success factors of an organization. These are usually a subset of the total metrics in the information security metrics program. They differ from an objective in that an objective is something you want to achieve, whereas a KPI is something used to verify if your efforts are leading you toward the defined objective. If KPIs are used as a matter of course across the organization (business or IT), then security-related KPIs may be identified as part of Step 4 mentioned earlier, or independently as a follow-on step if not consistently used by the business.

Examples of Strategic KPIs

- Percentage of business initiatives supported by the information security program (percentage of security supported business initiatives against total). The higher the value, the more optimized the information security resources, since management resources are being used over more aspects of the organization.
- Percentage of information security initiatives containing cost/benefit estimates program (percentage of security investments with financial value estimates against total). This indicator shows the organization's maturity on tracking security investment value realization. The higher the value, the more the decisions are based on financial facts.
- Percentage of agreements with information security clauses (percentage contracts issued with security standard clauses of total awarded). This indicator shows how services and products are incorporating information security aspects (e.g., service level agreements on availability, confidentiality, integrity, and continuity). The higher the value, the better supported your relationships with clients and suppliers are.

Examples of IT Risk Management KPIs

- Percentage of key information systems that have completed an annual risk assessment (percentage key systems that have completed an annual risk assessment of the total number of systems). This indicator provides a view of how many key networks, systems, or applications have been evaluated for their security posture.
- Percentage of key information systems that have completed an annual risk assessment and rated "unsatisfactory" (percentage key systems that have completed an annual risk assessment with an unfavorable rating of the total number of systems). This indicator provides a view of how

many key networks, systems, or applications have been evaluated for their security posture and found lacking.

- Percentage of critical vendors whose information security is assessed (percentage of critical vendors who have completed a risk assessment). This indicator reveals the security posture of key suppliers on whom the organization is dependent.

Examples of Operational Security KPIs

- Percentage of systems (workstations, laptops, servers) with latest antivirus/antispyware signatures (percentage of systems with latest antivirus/antispyware signatures or total system population). This indicator describes the ability to reduce outages or nonproductively due to malicious software disruption.
- Percentage of email messages with malicious software attachments stopped within measurement period (percentage of email spam messages stopped/detected of total email). This indicator describes the ability to reduce outages or nonproductively due to malicious software disruption.
- Percentage of employees who have completed annual information security awareness training (percentage completions of total number of employees). An indicator of employee understanding of security policies and procedures deemed critical (e.g., how to identify and report a security event).

EXTERNAL BENCHMARKING

Benchmarking is the process of comparing organizational processes and performance metrics to industry standards and best practices from other organizations, optimally organizations in the same industry and size. In fact, the use of metrics and statistics in isolation could create a false sense of security for an organization. The ability to benchmark and obtain some form rating against a comparable norm has been the goal of many organizations, particularly those involved in formation security intensive activities. It ensures that the organization is continually striving to improve its performance through learning. Benchmarking also opens minds to ideas from new sources within the same industry and other sectors. It is important to make sure that potential benchmarking partners are already tracking specific metrics or that can be easily derived from existing measures. Optimally, widespread industry acceptance would have to be achieved with agreement on the specific metrics to be used and interpretation of the metric framework standard (i.e., IOS/IEC or NIST).

As a project, the benchmarking purpose, objectives, and scope should be documented. This is a necessity for any project, particularly if sponsorship is needed. An executive sponsor will want to understand the benefits of the benchmarking exercise. Secondly, the benchmarking sample should be carefully selected. The project could select a sample of organizations whose performance is actually worse or better than that of its own organization simply because of different industry, size, or geographical region. Benchmarking data will be difficult to compare "apples to apples" in terms of a bad sample selection. Lastly, the organization should agree on the primary information security metrics as the basis of comparison. These comparisons will be valid only if the participating organizations in the study measures performance in exactly the same way, every time.

Once the benchmark is concluded and lessons learned have been formulated, similar to any metrics program, the organization should develop and communicate an action plan for the changes that it will need to make to realize improvements. These action plans should feed its performance improvement processes, just as the actions developed from the information security metrics efforts.

COMMON OBJECTIONS TO INFORMATION SECURITY METRICS PROGRAMS

The introduction of any new measurement program will inevitably face objections. Although some objections may be totally legitimate and require addressing them to accommodate the obstacle, other objectives may be based on organizational culture and addressed with change management techniques. One common objection is the concern that managers could be assessed against a new set of metrics how their departments and staff perform against a goal. There will be many outside the information security organization who will be involved in collecting data whose activities and functions will be measured. This is a very personal reaction, and can be resolved with some socialization on the benefits of the program with these reluctant managers. Other common objections to an information security metrics program are:

- Cost of implementation. The additional effort in establishing an information security metrics program will require incremental funding for both development and sustainment of the effort (e.g., labor and possibly software). The cost can be offset through the benefits of the program in the cost avoidance or efficiencies gained by the investment. For regulated entities, an information security metrics program may be mandated as part of a compliance program.
- Size of the organization. An information security metrics program, like any metrics program, may be perceived as unwarranted overhead for small to medium-sized businesses. Although this concern is valid,

most small to medium-sized businesses may grow and, if privately held, become publically traded. Management through metrics as an organizational discipline will be expected if not required.

It is important to overcome these objections with sensible arguments of the benefits of the program. It is equally important not to "water down" information security metrics that then become meaningless. The goal of setting information security metrics is to improve organizational performance. Metrics and targets should be challenging; it will provide more value than focusing on something that is easily achievable or is already being achieved.

SUMMARY

The decision to implement a program of metrics and measurements is not to be taken lightly. The quality of the results will be directly attributable to the integrity and accuracy of the raw information collected and the stated objectives of the metric framework. The use of standards-based metrics program can be designed to be implemented as part of the wider ranging information security management standard since companies need to ensure that their information-gathering infrastructure meets or exceeds compliance guidelines as well as industry-recognized standards. This will assist them to withstand scrutiny from auditors and accountants. The use of security metrics and measurements is likely to increase. If properly researched and implemented, they will prove to be a valuable resource for IT security officers and the company as a whole. They will also encourage best practice while ensuring regulatory compliance. If poorly implemented, however, they will provide only meaningless figures, which may result in infrastructure weaknesses and a false sense of security. For this reason effective policies and procedures must be the cornerstone for reliable security metrics and measurements.

ACTIONS

Identify stakeholder for the information security metrics program.

- The information security team should identify champions and gather support for the information security metrics program. These stakeholders are the intended audience of the reports generated by the metrics program and most likely the decision makers from whom direction and guidance is sought.

Define the information security metrics programs and goals.

- The metrics program's goals and objectives should be traceable to the overall organizational goals and objectives. An acceptable approach is to decompose the business value chain and identify the nodes on which information security shortfalls or gaps may influence a business impact to the overall business goal in its market orientation.

Establish information security business relationship framework.

■ Establish a business relationship management framework for information security and the business. Introduce the role of business information security officer or business information risk manager as an advisory and consulting function to assist the business to meet their information security objectives, goals, and requirements.

Decide which metrics to report.

■ Implement a tiered approach to address strategic decision making, risk management, and operational information security, each with specific metrics and targets for the various audiences.

Establish metric targets and thresholds.

■ To increase or maintain high levels of quality, organizations must set targets and performance thresholds at which corrective action must be taken.

Develop strategies for collecting metrics data.

■ Determine the sources of measures to be collected, how data will be collected (manual or automated), and how the data will be stored.

Determine how metrics will be reported.

■ Provide an easy-to-understand graphical representation of the collected information security metric.

Create a remediation action plan.

■ Ensure that any gap is addressed with a remediation plan that will close the gap or correct the concern.

Conduct a formal program review cycle.

■ Check the metrics program for relevancy and consistency on an annual basis.

Select KPIs

■ KPIs should be extrapolated from the various metrics being collected, down select to a few highly relevant, impactful performance indicators that represent the strategic, business, and operational goals of the program.

Conduct external benchmarking.

■ Information security leaders should avoid the tendency to be insular and myopic in the metrics program; look outward to identify best practices through peer comparisons.

Reference

[1] Ouedraogo M, Savola RM, Mouratidis H, et al. Taxonomy of quality metrics for assessing assurance of security correctness. Softw Qual J March 2013;21(1):67–97.

Index